Praise for *Near Enemies of the Truth*

"New age thinking often expresses an eternal truth that has subsequently been appropriated by the ego and used in service of its fears and desires. With characteristic insight and precision, Christopher Wallis takes many of the popular ideas that characterize new age, self-help culture, revealing the perennial truth on which they are founded whilst exposing the extent to which they have been distorted by popular thinking. *Near Enemies of the Truth* is like a Zen master's sword—both uncompromising and kind—and, as such, an invaluable companion to anyone who wishes to be scrupulously honest in their quest to recognize their essential nature and its inherent peace. I learned a lot from reading this book and thoroughly recommend it, as well as Christopher's work in general."

—Rupert Spira, spiritual teacher, philosopher, and author of *You Are the Happiness You Seek*

"The spiritual journey is replete with self-deception. The closer the deception is to our sense of self, the harder it is to recognize it. It's far easier to bypass the deception altogether! In *Near Enemies of the Truth*, beloved author Christopher Wallis skillfully and expertly explores the minute distinctions in concepts that appear to be the same but are vastly different and lead to different goals, often far away from the very thing we seek. It is a much-needed book for not just the world of spiritual seekers but for anyone interested in understanding their inner landscapes and arriving at peace and wisdom. I cannot recommend it enough!"

—Kavitha Chinnaiyan, MD, award-winning author of *Shakti Rising* and *Glorious Alchemy*

"*Near Enemies of the Truth* is a deliciously disruptive inoculation against BS teachings in the world of alternative spirituality. I wish this could be required reading for all 'spiritual teachers.'"

—Harshada David Wagner, meditation teacher, spiritual coach, and author of *Backbone*

Near Enemies of the Truth

Avoid the Pitfalls of the Spiritual Life and Become Radically Free

Christopher D. Wallis, PhD

WONDERWELL

Library of Congress Control Number: 2023910356

ISBN 978-1-63756-037-2
eISBN 978-1-63756-038-9

Editor: Allison Serrell
Cover and interior design: Debbie Berne
Author photograph: Stuart Williams

Published by Wonderwell in Los Angeles, CA
www.wonderwell.press

Produced in partnership with Mattamayūra Press

Distributed in the US by Publishers Group West and in Canada by Publishers Group Canada.

Printed and bound in Canada

23 24 25 26   5 4 3 2 1

dedicated to the truth

Contents

Introduction

OF ALL THE ASPECTS OF HUMAN LIFE, spirituality holds the greatest potential for fulfillment, and yet it can also be deeply problematic. It offers the possibility of more profound paradigm shifts than any other domain of human life and the possibility of becoming profoundly confused and deluded. If the spiritual life is more than just a hobby for you, then the stakes are high—perhaps even higher than you realize.

If you can navigate around psychological pitfalls on the spiritual path, it can facilitate incredible joy and freedom. But that's a big if. Many people have never been taught how to navigate around these pitfalls, and as a result, they sometimes end up in strange, isolating cul-de-sacs from which they might not emerge in this life. We've all seen examples of gurus who were once genuine teachers but who became delusional over time and ended up causing great harm to their followers. This phenomenon is just as common among spiritual practitioners who are not gurus, though negative effects are, of course, less obvious.

The perils and promise of the spiritual life are both very real. I have experienced both in abundance in my own practice and in the lives of my teachers and friends. It is that hard-earned firsthand knowledge that prompted me to write this book.

One note here on the nature of the spiritual life. On this journey, it is crucial to distinguish between *religion* and *spirituality*: we can say that the former consists of comforting beliefs (and thus, if we're honest, much of what people today call spirituality is actually religion), and the latter consists of the willingness to strip away beliefs to see what's really true. The purpose of this book is to support you in that spiritual endeavor.

Though this book offers itself to you as a guide to the pitfalls of the spiritual life, it doesn't focus on the negative. In each chapter, after pointing out how a spiritual teaching can be construed in a harmful way, I focus on the deeper truth of that teaching, which is often obscured by its popular bumper sticker version. Each chapter contains supportive insights for your spiritual process and everyday life, as well as guidance for avoiding the pitfalls adjacent to that insight. Several chapters include a suggested meditation to help you more deeply explore the topic.

What qualifies me to write such a book, you might ask. I have been studying and practicing Asian forms of spirituality for over thirty years. I've earned four university degrees in classical Indian religions (Buddhism, Hinduism, etc.), but those academic qualifications are not as important for this book as my years of practical engagement with the spiritual path, and the years of observing various spiritual communities prosper—and go off the rails. For the past several years, I've been building and guiding a worldwide community, which is an absolute dream come true: caring, truly mature adults supporting one another on the path. It took years of teaching experience, and years of working on myself and coaching people from many different cultures, to become confident about what really facilitates human flourishing and to see that confidence repeatedly validated.

Who is this book for? If you're reading these words, it's probably for you. The assumed audience, however, consists of people who have practiced, or are interested in, meditation and mindfulness—that is, people who have engaged to some degree with forms of spirituality derived from Asia and/or forms of alternative Western spirituality sometimes designated as "New Age" (which are influenced in varying degrees by Asian spiritual teachings).

What Are Near Enemies of the Truth?

The title of this book might initially be confusing. In modern Buddhism, near enemies are defined as "states that appear *similar* to the desired quality but actually undermine it," as opposed to far enemies, which are simply the opposite of what we hope to cultivate or achieve.* Buddhist teacher Jack Kornfield writes, "The near enemies depict how spirituality can be misunderstood or misused to separate us from life," and in referring to this quote, author Brené Brown rightly points out, "What's interesting is that near enemies are often greater threats than far enemies because they're more difficult to recognize."** That is the key. We need books like Brown's and the one you're holding because we need help recognizing the near enemies, since they are so often disguised as desirable qualities or valid spiritual teachings but are off the mark in ways that really matter.

In modern Buddhism, near enemies are usually simple concepts, such as "The near enemy of compassion is pity" or "The near

---

*Chris Germer, "The Near and Far Enemies of Fierce Compassion," Center for Mindful Self-Compassion, September 2, 2020, centerformsc.org/the-near-and-far-enemies-of-fierce-compassion.

**Brené Brown, *Atlas of the Heart: Mapping Meaningful Connection and the Language of Human Experience* (New York: Random House, 2021), 118, Kindle. Brown amplifies this by saying that "the near enemies of emotions or experiences might look and even feel like connection, but ultimately they drive us to be disconnected from ourselves and from each other. Without awareness, near enemies become the practices that fuel separation, rather than practices that reinforce the inextricable connection of all people." (Brown, 252), which also cites the Jack Kornfield quote, derived from his book Bringing Home the Dharma: Awakening Right Where You Are (Boston: Shambhala, 2011), 102.

enemy of love is attachment." In other words, pity is easily mistaken for compassion, or attachment for love, but the former doesn't yield the benefits of those latter virtues. In this book, I seek to show that the near enemies teaching can be much more powerful by offering a more detailed and nuanced version of it. This book argues that nearly all the popular spiritual platitudes found in alternative spiritual communities (and sometimes in mainstream religion as well) constitute near enemies of the truth.

In this definition, near enemies are distorted or oversimplified versions of some of the most significant yet subtle spiritual insights developed over the ages. They are statements that are close to a profound and subtle truth but are distorted just enough to lead one significantly astray in the long run, resulting in needless suffering. When we're talking about deep and fundamental truths, getting it a little bit wrong doesn't much matter in the short term, but it very much matters in the long term—just like a tiny adjustment to the rudder of your boat makes little difference at first, but after two thousand miles, it lands you on a different continent.

Now, some people object to the use of the word *wrong* in the previous sentence, subscribing as they do to the idea that the *only* necessary criterion for truth is "It feels true to me." This view can be as dangerous in spirituality as it is in politics. It can lead to states of delusion that feel good initially but that severely undermine our capacity to flourish in the long term. With this book, I wish to convince you that understanding the near enemies of the truth, and specifically why they are near enemies and not the truth itself, is hugely important for any spiritual aspirant who wants to get past beginner stages and into deep (and deeply fulfilling) spiritual work.

Having said that, it's important to note that if a near enemy is near enough, it can actually be a *temporary ally*—something very helpful on your journey but only for a limited time, until you develop a more mature understanding. If you skim the chapter titles of this book, such as "Listen to Your Heart," "Love Yourself," and "Everything

Happens for a Reason," I bet you'll find that some of these near enemies have been temporary allies for you. I'm not disputing the great value these statements might have had for you in the past. But as one progresses on the path, and the stakes get higher in one's spiritual practice, there is no such thing as "close enough" anymore, and your comforting affirmations must be sacrificed on the altar of truth—otherwise, your spiritual progress stalls. Of course, you don't yet see why these statements are merely adjacent to the truth rather than simply true. That's why you're reading this book. The willingness to challenge what we think we know is indispensable on the spiritual path, and I commend you for it.

Why I Wrote This Book

Over the years, I've spent time in various spiritual communities, from traditional Hindu and Buddhist communities to so-called New Age communities. In this time, I became increasingly concerned with the role platitudes played in these communities and how they often took the place of the challenging but rewarding work of deep inner contemplation. In the most egregious examples (which were commonplace in my experience), people used these platitudes (disguised as wisdom, of course) to avoid facing difficult issues or doing emotional work, despite the great benefits of that work. For example, if "Everything happens for the best" and "You create your own reality," then I can't be held accountable for whatever you think I did to you. This is called *spiritual bypassing,* and it can be quite harmful to one's relationships and inhibit the process of real spiritual awakening.

I also became concerned about the increasing prevalence of what philosophers call relativism—the stance that everyone's point of view is equally valid. Though on the surface this sounds like a pleasingly tolerant idea, unfortunately the only way everyone's point of view can be equally valid is when there is no such thing as truth. Thus, relativism always masks an implicit nihilism (the view that there are no fundamental truths), and nihilism tends to make human beings cynical and deeply dissatisfied, even when implicit.

These concerns were exacerbated by the changes in US society over the last seven or eight years, a time in which the endemic American distrust of experts and expertise peaked, leading many to suspect that there were no such things as facts in any realm apart from hard science (or even in that realm!), let alone truth. Needless to say, when the idea of truth itself is open to question, the near enemies of the truth flourish like weeds in an untended garden.

This book takes the stance that there *are* fundamental truths that can be verified through careful contemplation of your own experience. Indeed, if there weren't fundamental truths pertaining to the human experience of reality, truths that impinge upon us whether we're aware of them or not, we would never be able to effectively communicate or authentically connect with one another.

The modern spiritual marketplace and self-help industry, unfortunately, is rife with near enemies of the truth, because people are inclined toward material that validates and elaborates on what they already believe. The system we have includes no economic incentives for the discovery of truth, especially when the process of discovery is difficult or uncomfortable, even if it eventually results in great joy.

Social media has exacerbated the problem further, as the platitudes peddled by self-help gurus get endlessly repeated as various kinds of memes. And the more someone's heard a specific cliché repeated as gospel within their community, the less likely they are to question it.

My heartfelt wish is that this book may effectively show why and how these platitudes can be harmful, and how grasping the deeper truths to which they are adjacent is profoundly liberating. You, dear reader, are presented now with an opportunity: Will you walk with me for a bit as I challenge some of your beliefs, and perhaps even skewer some of your sacred cows, if I assure you that the result will be a more nuanced and revitalized spiritual life?

Where I'm Coming From

My educational background is in the field of comparative religion, which involves studying the various religious traditions of the world both on their own terms and through comparing them. My specialty is South Asian philosophy, religion, and spirituality. (The geographical term *South Asia* covers the whole of the Indian subcontinent, the religious culture of which was disproportionately influential on the rest of Asia all the way up to the modern period.) The area of my greatest expertise is the spiritual tradition of Tantric Shaivism, also known as Shaiva Tantra, which flourished in all parts of the Indian subcontinent and many parts of Southeast Asia about a thousand years ago. The domain of Tantric Shaivism significantly overlaps with that of Tantric Buddhism, best known to the contemporary world in its Tibetan form, popularized by Tibetan Buddhist teachers like the Dalai Lama.

Both Shaiva Tantra and Buddhist Tantra, in their most developed and sophisticated forms, seek to transcend their religious background (Hinduism and Buddhism, respectively) and therefore teach methods for immersing oneself in the nonconceptual direct experience of reality as such. Studying and practicing these methods have been my passion for many years. In this book, I seek to synthesize various elements of my educational and practical background, thereby combining an understanding of those principles of spiritual insight that are more or less universal across different cultural environments with the specific insights of classical Tantra in its most developed forms.*

---

*Some object to the use of the word *classical* in this context, seeing it as part of a rhetorical strategy designed to elevate the speaker's voice and intentionally

These great spiritual traditions have worked to refine their pointers toward the truth over the course of centuries. When such a treasure trove of wisdom is available to us, why should we be satisfied with near enemies or even temporary allies instead of the finest jewels of wisdom? The further we go on the spiritual path, the greater and more precise our discernment and understanding must be. This is both because spiritual practice generates power and energy that requires greater discernment to deploy nonharmfully and because the spiritual path seeks to free us from our cultural programming, and without precise discernment and wisdom guiding that process, we can walk perilously close to the edge of madness.

With that introduction to the topic, let's now turn to the near enemies treated in this book and the contemplation of those ineffable truths hidden by them. We begin in Part One with those near enemies that are more innocuous and relatively easy to grasp when pointed out and progress to those that are more insidious and more difficult to grasp (and explain!) due to their subtlety. Furthermore, in Part Two, we go beyond near enemies per se and explore key spiritual concepts that when understood superficially become near enemies, but when engaged on a deeper level are instrumental to spiritual awakening.

---

or unintentionally erase indigenous vernacular traditions that might be seen as nonclassical. But I use the word simply to denote a specific body of literature—that is, the literature written in Sanskrit during the period of greatest flourishing of the Tantric traditions, the tenth and eleventh centuries CE. This literature had a profound influence on Indic thought in the second millennium as well as, indirectly, on the teachings woven through much of the modern postural yoga scene today.

PART ONE

NAVIGATING RIPTIDES

NEAR ENEMY #1

Follow Your Bliss

THE 1960S GAVE US AN IDEAL of doing what we love, bucking the system, following our heart's path, making our own way, and becoming successful on our own terms. But the '60s also gave us a legacy of profound disillusionment, disaffection, and widespread drug addiction. Why this contradiction? While the maxim of that decade, "Do what you love and the money will follow," appeared to work, it was often because of a booming economy and other forms of privilege and advantage. The hippie ethos of the '60s gave way to the New Age movement of the '70s, '80s, and beyond, which spoke of a "law of attraction" by which we could manifest the life of our dreams by simply thinking positive thoughts and vividly envisioning our success. This philosophy has a significant dark side, though: if it's true that your success depends on nothing but you and the power of your mind, then lack of success must be proof positive that you're simply not good enough, which for many is their worst fear and their darkest thought. On the other hand, if you believe in this philosophy and you *are* successful (according to the standards of modern capitalism), it serves to aggrandize your ego to the detriment of your relationships.

Many hyper-capitalist Boomers of today were the long-haired idealists of yesteryear, and most of their children and grandchildren still believe that success consists of fame (e.g., social media followers) and money, and that they're entitled to those things while doing whatever they most like.

Though many of us like to believe we're evolving as a species and as a society, there's no evidence that people today are any happier, on average, than fifty years ago. Could this be because our principles and values, as a society, have remained relatively superficial and unexamined? This book seeks to re-examine some of the maxims and platitudes that people in spiritual communities and in the wider culture often try to live by. Through such careful examination, I hope to show that a deeper and more nuanced understanding of these principles can lead to a much greater sense of well-being, regardless of one's circumstances. Everyone knows that the spiritual traditions of the East teach that happiness is found within, not in quantifiable attributes like followers and financial figures, but that idea remains hollow unless someone can show you exactly *how* to find happiness within yourself. You must reconsider and replace some deep-seated assumptions and subtle misunderstandings to clear the way to the wellspring of well-being within. This book aspires to help you do that.

The idea "Do what you love and the money will follow," also commonly phrased as "Follow your bliss and the money will come," was an unfortunate distortion of the teaching of the influential psychologist and mythologist Joseph Campbell, who wrote *The Hero with a Thousand Faces* and *The Power of Myth*. I grew up with his teachings, because in the 1980s, my father designed and facilitated unique interactive events for kids ages ten through twelve based on Campbell's work. Campbell's concept of the hero's journey as a cross-cultural map of the spiritual path was an influence on my still-forming brain.

Campbell followed in the footsteps of his Indology professor, the great Heinrich Zimmer, in studying the spiritual traditions of India (though he did not master Sanskrit as Zimmer did). In contemplative meditation on the Sanskrit compound *saccidānanda* (a Vedantic description of the nature of ultimate reality in terms of *sat* [being], *cit* [consciousness], and *ānanda* [bliss or rapture]), Campbell realized that he didn't know the true nature of his being or his consciousness, but he knew what rapture was, so he decided to follow that. In this moment of insight, he intuited (correctly, I would say) that successful contemplative investigation of any one of the three elements would lead to an understanding of the other two.*

As a result, he coined the phrase "Follow your bliss," which in his usage diverged from the original Vedantic contemplation and came to mean something like "Do what you love," a usage likely influenced by the essays of Carl Jung and Walter Pater. The hippie movement appropriated Campbell's phrase and inflected it further to mean something like "Do whatever feels good." But Campbell meant something different. He was suggesting that we follow the thread of our passion wherever it leads, despite any heartache along the way. A story circulates that, late in life, Campbell joked, "I should have said 'follow your blisters'!" While this quote may well be apocryphal (since I was unable to trace it), there exists a good reason for its fabrication: given the context of the primarily Boomer-age audience which received it, Campbell's famous phrase would have been less misunderstood had he said "Pursue your passion," since the word *passion* in English connotes suffering almost as much as it connotes love. And Campbell certainly understood that doing what you most love might not be easy, and might not make you any money, as exemplified in this quote:

---

*"Now, I came to this idea of bliss because in Sanskrit, which is the great spiritual language of the world, there are three terms that represent the brink, the jumping-off place to the ocean of transcendence: *sat-chit-ānanda*. The word 'Sat' means being. 'Chit' means consciousness. 'Ānanda' means bliss or rapture. I thought, 'I don't know whether my consciousness is proper consciousness or not; I don't know whether what I know of my being is my proper being or not; but I do know where my rapture is. So let me hang on to rapture, and that will bring me both my consciousness and my being." Joseph Campbell, *The Power of Myth* (New York: Anchor, 1991), 120.

> The adventure is its own reward—but it's necessarily dangerous, having both negative and positive possibilities, all of them beyond [our] control. We are following our own way, not our daddy's or our mother's way . . . There's something inside you that knows when you're in the center, that knows when you're on the beam or off the beam. And if you get off the beam to earn money, you've lost your life. And if you stay in the center and don't get any money, you still have your bliss.
>
> If you follow your bliss, you put yourself on a kind of track that has been there all the while, waiting for you, and [then] the life that you ought to be living is the one you are living. When you can see that, you begin to meet people who are in the field of your bliss, and they open doors to you. I say, follow your bliss and don't be afraid, and doors will open where you didn't know they were going to be.*

The teaching here is clear—it's not "Do whatever feels good, and you'll be happy in life." Campbell tells us that following our bliss is potentially dangerous because we may enter uncharted territory—but it is simultaneously inherently worthwhile because "The adventure is its own reward." The adventure he speaks of is what unfolds when we orient toward our heart's deepest longing (whether or not we understand it) and do that which feels most deeply right and true in our life, whatever the cost. But we cannot sense our heart's deepest longing or what feels right and true unless we learn how to deeply listen to the whole of our experience without agenda.

True meditation is nothing but the cultivation of our capacity to deeply listen in this way.** Through listening—not with the ears but with our whole being—we arrive at a quiet inner knowing of

*Campbell, *The Power of Myth*, 113.

**As taught in Adyashanti's wonderful book *True Meditation*.

what is right for us, which is not obtainable through any amount of thinking or discussing with others (though those activities can sometimes be valuable as well, especially if you have wise beings in your life that can offer well-grounded reflection). When we experience this quiet inner knowing, we can begin to align our thoughts, words, and actions with it. The more we bring about this alignment, the more fully and freely we can access our natural capacity for joy. This is what it means to follow your bliss.

Campbell chose the word *bliss* rather than *passion* because he was originally inspired by the Sanskrit word *ānanda,* which is certainly closer to the first English word than the second. But ānanda is not really translatable since it refers not to extreme happiness but a kind of quiet joy in aliveness itself that is not contingent on circumstance. This kind of joy, this ānanda, is not produced by getting what you want; rather, it is an inherent capacity of consciousness that can be accessed much more effectively by simply being, with full awareness-presence, than by doing anything, however pleasurable. In the Tantric tradition, there is a teaching of seven levels of ānanda because, as it turns out, the experience of ānanda can deepen and become infused into every aspect of one's everyday life—but only when you have spent years aligning the actions of body, speech, and mind with what your innermost intuition feels is deeply right and true. Needless to say, this must include either bringing your professional work into the same alignment, or if that proves impossible, relinquishing it to make room for work that is aligned (or alignable).

When we accurately understand the inner meaning of "Follow your bliss," we see that it is the same teaching as found in this phrase of Rumi's as rendered by Coleman Barks: "Let yourself be silently drawn by the strange pull of what you truly love. It will not lead you astray."* (*Strange* in the sense of "mysterious," here.) This phrase

---

*Barks has rendered this line in more than one way in the different editions of *The Essential Rumi.* Another edition has: "Let yourself be silently drawn by the stronger pull of what you really love."

from Barks's Rumi is beautiful and deeply resonant, but since the word *love* is just as open to misinterpretation as *bliss*, I often prefer to call this teaching "following the golden thread."

To explain: when a meditation practice is engaged as an opportunity to become more grounded in the real rather than a kind of spiritual escapism in which you seek to dissociate from your life, and when—from that grounded, clear, calm, eyes-wide-open state—you learn to pay attention to the whole of your experience, you perceive something like a tapestry of countless threads, all beautifully and inextricably interwoven, including the threads of your pain and joy, and every pair of apparent opposites. As you continue to pay attention, you notice that somewhere in the tapestry of your experience there is a tiny golden thread sticking out, subtly gleaming. Your intuition points you toward it. That golden thread could be a simple intuition to read a particular book, sit with a particular teacher, accept a particular invitation, call a particular friend, or visit a particular place—anything. It subtly gleams. It appears quietly, without demands, just feeling right. You can ignore it, or you can gently tug on that golden thread. Once you start pulling it, it leads you somewhere, which leads you somewhere else, and so on. And if you follow it to all the places (both literal and metaphorical, but usually the latter) it leads you, you discover exactly where it is that you've been this whole time. As the poet says, "With the drawing of this Love and the voice of this Calling / We shall not cease from exploration / And the end of all our exploring / Will be to arrive where we started / And know the place for the first time."* In this way, you find your true home in the very heart of existence.

Following the golden thread is indeed following your bliss because it inevitably leads to a state in which you have more access to the innate joy of being. But the journey is sometimes anything but blissful. As the poet Kahlil Gibran wrote in *The Prophet*, "When

*Eliot, T.S., "Little Gidding" in *Four Quartets.*

Love beckons to you, follow him, though his ways are hard and steep." However, if you glimpse that the spiritual journey inevitably unveils nothing less than the very reason for being, the truth of existence, the infinite majesty of your own innate divinity expressed in the whole of reality, you do not hesitate to walk the path presented to you in each moment. To truly follow your bliss means that you would willingly pay any price, bear any burden, meet any hardship, support any truth, and discard any falsehood to realize and abide in your true nature and align everything in your life to it.

Having begun this chapter on a personal note, I'll end on one. I was fortunate enough to orient my life to this teaching and start following my bliss more than twenty-four years ago, when I heeded the inner call to study South Asian religions full time and enrolled as a university freshman at the "late" age of twenty-five. My intention was to study these spiritual traditions in depth to offer their wisdom to others. Ever since I made that decision, I fell onto a life path in which I was supported at every turn as long as I stayed on that track. Everything in my life unfolded with seemingly unerring perfection as long as I remembered to listen to the whole of my experience and remain open to discern the intuitive clues as to what was next. Many times, I forgot to listen and got caught in my own mind games. But as my sense of contracted separate self was slowly eroded by spiritual practice, listening became easier and easier and my fear of completely trusting life became less and less. My experience absolutely corroborates Campbell's statement: "If you follow your bliss, you put yourself on a kind of track that has been there all the while, waiting for you . . . Wherever you are—if you are following your bliss, you are enjoying that refreshment, that life within you, all the time."

If you can truly follow your bliss, the notion of "finding your soul's purpose" (discussed in a later chapter) becomes irrelevant. You will experience fulfillment each and every day in the dance of existence, and you know in your bones there is no higher purpose to be found, and none needed.

NEAR ENEMY #2

Speak Your Truth

IN THIS DAY AND AGE, truth is a slippery concept indeed. Many people are proudly "speaking their truth," which seems like a problematic thing to do without first establishing what truth is. Most people seem to be under the impression that truth is relative: what's true for me might not be true for you, and vice versa. I argue that this idea conflates truth with belief. We each form a belief or narrative about an event or a series of events, and those narratives are unlikely to match. But, insofar as these distinct narratives make claims about our shared reality, they cannot be equally true since truth is the property of being in accord with fact or reality.

As discussed in the introduction, I propose that in contrast to belief, truth is, by its very nature, indisputable. While we might dispute the validity of a method used to find truth, if two different but equally valid methods are used, they will yield the same result. For example, if one person measures the Eiffel Tower in meters and another person measures it in yards, the first will find that the tower is 324 meters tall and the second will find that it is 354.33 yards—but these two numbers describe the exact same length according to two different measuring systems.

There are two types of inarguable truths: subjective and objective. Objective truths are those we can all agree on if we bother to check, such as the height of the Eiffel Tower, the number of minutes between sunrise and sunset on a given day in a given location, and whether the number of reported violent crimes has increased or decreased in the past decade (FYI, it's decreased by 9 percent in the United States).* Subjective truths are known only to the one experiencing them (like what you dreamed last night or whether you have a pain in your knee right now) and are inarguable on that basis. (While anyone might be lying about their subjective experience, we can't know for sure that they are lying, and hence their testimony should be treated as inarguable unless we have a sufficiently compelling reason to suspect deceit.)

Truth or Interpretation?

Surprisingly, though the difference between truth and interpretation is very clear to anyone who thinks it through, people mix them up all the time. Further confusion is introduced by the fact that many people don't realize that a belief is not a truth of any kind—it's (at best) an interpretation of subjective and/or objective truths. An interpretation can be subjected to scrutiny and, because of that scrutiny, can be shown to correspond to the facts of the matter more or less closely; but even when an interpretation does a great job of making sense out of the facts, it still can't be considered truth per se—it's just a more effective way of thinking about something.

Human relations become profoundly fraught, if not actually violent, when people confuse these three categories: subjective truth,

*Federal Bureau of Investigation, "Crime in the United States 2019," 2019, ucr.fbi.gov/crime-in-the-u.s/2019/crime-in-the-u.s.-2019.

objective truth, and interpretation. The first two are inarguable, and the third not only is arguable but can be debated indefinitely. I propose that a clear understanding of the difference of these three categories renders human relations as harmonious as they can possibly be. I invite you to put this hypothesis to the test.

Let's explore some examples. People who believe their thoughts (i.e., most everyone) tend to speak their thoughts as if they were objective truths, something that they have observed. For example, one person might say to another, "You don't want me here." However, the inarguable truth of the matter might be "You're not paying as much attention to me as I would like, and so I'm thinking that you don't want me here, and I'm tending toward believing that thought, so I'm feeling pretty sad right now." See the difference? The second statement is inarguable, and the first is not. The second statement is inarguable precisely because it characterizes the speaker's experience rather than the interiority of the other person. Truth versus interpretation.

Confusion easily arises on this point because of the way language works. English, like many other languages, possesses something called the past passive participle, a word that usually functions as a verbal adjective (such as many English words ending in *-ed,* like disrespected, attacked, betrayed, judged, praised, etc.) Any judgment of another person's behavior can be disguised as a first-person statement of one's own feeling, such as in the statement "I feel disrespected," where the participle *disrespected* denotes not an emotion but an evaluation of the other person's behavior: "I feel disrespected (by you)" is often a sneaky way of making the claim "You disrespected me." This is hardly an inarguable statement, so it is very likely to get you into an argument. Such a statement judgmentally stands in for the inarguable truth of the matter, which is, in this instance, probably something like *I feel sad and angry because I want you to give greater importance to my feelings, needs, and values than you currently are, in my perception.* Judgments and evaluations don't help us understand each other, connect, or heal. Inarguable truth statements do.

One needs to exercise great discernment to make truly inarguable statements. The example italicized sentence adds the phrase *in my perception* at the end because otherwise your interlocutor can respond, "But I am giving importance to your feelings, needs, and values!" thereby missing the point. Adding *in my perception* emphasizes that you are lacking a felt-sense that the other person attributes significance to your feelings, needs, and values. You want that person to behave in such a way that you can palpably feel that they give importance to your needs and values, so this is what you need to communicate. What is inarguable in this scenario is the fact that you currently cannot sense that they are giving importance to your feelings and needs to the degree that you wish, and perhaps not even to the degree that would make you feel truly safe in relating with that person.

One needs to exercise great discernment to make truly inarguable statements.

If you want to communicate and connect effectively, whenever you say, "I feel __________," make sure you fill in the blank with an actual emotion, not a disguised evaluation of the other person's actions. "Betrayed" is not an emotion—"angry" is. "Disrespected" is not an emotion—"sad" is. If someone says, "I feel disrespected," that's usually a way of disguising the belief or claim "You disrespected me." I say "usually" because someone might use the phrase "I feel disrespected" to mean "I can't say whether you disrespected me or not, but your words landed that way for me," but such usage is all too rare compared to that of the disguised evaluation or judgment. The word *feel* is nowadays often used to denote what one believes to be a valid description of the other's actions.

But here's the thing: each of us can only articulate truth from a first-person perspective ("I"), not a second-person perspective ("you"). A statement beginning with the word *you* (that is, an evaluation of a situation with a second-person subject), whether explicit or disguised, often presumes to characterize, label, or evaluate someone else's actions or experience or perspective, which is not something we're in a legitimate position to do (with the possible exception of a skilled mental health professional). It's impossible to make a truth statement when you're characterizing someone else's subjective experience or perspective unless you clearly label it as a speculation (such as "I'm guessing that you're feeling upset about what I said" or "I'm imagining that you betrayed me").

Inarguable Truths

The principles outlined so far are important to understand thoroughly, so let's look at a few more examples in which we translate arguable judgments into inarguable truth statements:

- "You're being very disrespectful" might mean "I find it frustrating when you interrupt me, and it makes it hard for me to believe that you respect my opinion."
- "Immigrants can't be trusted" might mean "I've had bad experiences with a couple of people who didn't speak my language very well, so I find myself feeling nervous around people who look or sound like them."
- "Trump voters are stupid" might mean "When I listen to the rationales given by people explaining why they voted for Trump, I never seem to find them compelling or persuasive."
- "You don't care about me!" might mean "Based on behaviors X and Y (objective inarguables), my mind's telling me the story that you don't care about me, and right now I'm having a hard time disbelieving it."
- "I'm such an idiot, I'll never be good enough" might mean "When people are angry with me and say I should have behaved differently, I'm filled with shame and discouraged

about whether I'll be able to please them or live up to their expectations."

Now, if you're still subject to mainstream cultural programming, then it's likely that the second statements in each bullet point, despite being much more honest and accurate, make you roll your eyes a bit. But it's precisely this prejudice we have against being open, honest, and scrupulously accurate in our statements that leads to conflict and suffering in our relationships. If we can learn to speak using true and inarguable first-person statements, rather than arguable interpretations focused on the second or third persons (*you* and *they*), it can radically transform our relationships for the better.

Now I'll attempt to address an issue that often arises when we seek the truth in these interpersonal contexts. For example, when someone who is habitually reticent to speak up asserts firmly—e.g., "You're being very disrespectful!"—to someone they perceive as aggressive, we are tempted to applaud for them, and rightly so, in one sense. It's wonderful that they're learning to assert themselves. But they're not actually speaking truth, since *disrespectful* is an interpretation of the facts, not a fact itself, however well justified one thinks the interpretation is. (Note that what is considered respectful behavior varies from culture to culture; for example, interrupting is not considered rude in Italy, but it is in Japan.) We cannot base our assessment of the truth-value of any statement on how much sympathy or empathy we feel with the speaker, or we lose sight of what truth means.

If our assertive hypothetical person simply wishes to feel the pleasure of telling the other person off, then proclaiming their evaluation of the person is just fine. But if they hope for improved relations with their interlocutor on an ongoing basis, they will need to speak more skillfully, using inarguable first-person statements, as exemplified above. When a person perceives themselves as being criticized, the most common response is an immediate defense: "I was just joking!" Or a dismissal: "Don't be so sensitive." As long as they're defending themselves, they're not listening to you or connecting with your lived experience.

In my view, there's nothing more important for successful interpersonal relationships than this. If we can speak in actual inarguables, authentically undeniable truths, we rapidly get to the heart of the matter and have a productive conversation instead of wasting mental and emotional energy on endlessly disputing arguable interpretations.* Here's an example of a statement full of inarguables that is likely to result in effective communication and human connection:

> When I walked into the kitchen this morning and saw the stack of dirty dishes in the sink [objective inarguable], my heart sank [subjective inarguable]. It's so important to me to walk into a clean kitchen in the morning [subjective statement of value, also inarguable], and I began to worry that that need of mine wasn't likely to be met [subjective inarguable]. Would you be willing to commit to doing your dishes before going to bed every night [specific actionable request]?**

Of course, rather than following this example as written, it's important to make the language natural to your way of speaking while still using inarguable first-person statements. Now let's contrast the above paragraph to how these conversations usually go down.

---

*Please note, however, that in the phenomenon now known as *gaslighting,* someone may in fact deny your experience even when you are using inarguable statements. If you experience this repeatedly with someone, and you are indeed using inarguable statements, that person should be considered hazardous to your mental-emotional health. Another, even more insidious, form of gaslighting is when someone seeks to undermine the other person's accurate intuition about something through systematic denials and statements that imply that the other person is delusional.

**In real-life situations, I recommend more interpersonal exchanges before getting to the request.

A: What's bugging you?

B: I'm tired of living with someone who doesn't care about my needs, that's all.

A: What are you talking about?

B: You're always leaving the kitchen a mess! Why are you such a slob? Don't you care about other people? Can you please have some f***ing consideration?

A: Jesus, you're one to talk! You're always on my case! Why don't you stop being such an anal clean freak and consider the fact that I might have a need to be left in peace for once?

They could not be more different. Using inarguable statements is not only more aligned with truth but also results in a higher likelihood that one's needs get met. This is because of the Satya principle (common to both Yoga and Buddhism), which states that in real life (not the movies), truth is always the most effective long-term strategy for meeting one's needs—if only one can discern what truth actually is.

"I" Statements

I recommend that you get obsessed for a while with clearly differentiating objective and subjective truths and making sure both are expressed using inarguable statements. This can save you from enormous heartache and headaches. You might want to test your statements out on a friend who's in on the game before using them with the person they concern. Remember, objective truths are things everyone with first-hand experience of the matter can agree on (discounting those who argue in bad faith, a phenomenon sadly on the rise). Subjective truths, which are often more important for human flourishing than objective ones, are individual truths represented in "I" statements, and they fall into the following categories:

- Sensations
- Feelings
- Needs
- Desires
- Values

Unfortunately, most people have an impoverished vocabulary in all these areas. "Most people" likely includes you, so I strongly recommend you develop your vocabulary in the areas of feelings, needs, and values. Otherwise, you are very likely to end up expressing a judgment or evaluation when you're trying to express a feeling or need.

With all my heart, I implore you to realize that judging, diagnosing, labeling, or pathologizing another person is not speaking your truth. Characterizing another person's experience, feelings, needs, or values is not speaking your truth. Your truth, by definition, is precisely that arena that is unknowable to others: your sensations, feelings, needs, desires, and values. And it should go without saying that your opinion about something verifiable or falsifiable in the domain of shared reality is not "your truth." Thoughts and opinions that relate to and impinge on our shared experience are up for debate, without exception. And some opinions can be shown to be more valid than others because they are better supported by the evidence. It's simply not the case that everyone's equally entitled to their opinion. Everyone is entitled to think what they like, but as soon as they express an opinion, they are offering it into the arena of shared discourse, and it becomes part of our communal struggle to find intersubjective truths. Your opinion, once expressed, is not your truth but part of our collective search for intersubjective meaning.*

In conclusion, I invite you to pause, breathe, and reflect before speaking on any emotionally charged issue. Ask yourself, What can you know to be true about the situation? What are the objective inarguables and the subjective inarguables? And what are your thoughts, intuitions, desires, and fears concerning the other person? It's okay to share any of those, as long as your thoughts or intuitions are honestly labeled as such. ("You haven't told me how you're feeling, but my intuition tells me you're mad at me—can you tell me if that's true?") So many needless arguments are avoided if we cultivate the humility needed to avoid the assumption that our thoughts, intuitions, and suspicions are correct, and get curious about the other person's inner world, about how they perceive and interpret things (while, of course, suspending judgment about the validity of such interpretations).

May we all have the courage to be loyal to truth and the humility to admit how much we don't know for sure. May we speak the truth as far as we can discern it using the tools available to us while remaining open to hearing the other person's experience. And may all beings benefit!**

---

*Intersubjective meaning is exemplified by categories like justice and morality: these are neither objective truths embedded in the nature of reality per se, nor are they individual subjective truths (since anyone who thinks they can determine their own morality and justice without reference to the human collective is deemed mentally ill). Though justice, morality, money, and nations are fictions that are rewritten over time, they have tremendous power because of their *intersubjective* truth, sometimes called "the social contract." For more on this, see Yuval Harari's *Sapiens* among many other sources.

**Thanks to the late great Marshall Rosenberg for inspiring so much of this chapter. He was a peerless exemplar of always speaking truth infused with compassion.

CONTEMPLATIVE EXERCISE

What Is the Truth of My Experience?

—

Get settled and take a few deep breaths. Let go of all your stories, your interpretations, and your opinions for now. Let go of any urgency, any sense that something needs to be done. Continue breathing a little deeper than usual and just be with your experience without labeling it. Now, when you turn your attention to a situation that's been challenging for you, simply notice what happens in your body. Be with it compassionately. Then ask yourself what you need in this situation or what you are longing for. Let go of any judgment around this need or longing. Just acknowledge it and be with it. Whatever you need and want is natural for you; it's not wrong. Notice that your truth lies only in the domain of your own experience: your feelings, wants, needs, and values. Resolve to speak that truth whenever others are open to hearing it.

NEAR ENEMY #3

Be Your Best Self

THE SELF-HELP INDUSTRY has perpetuated the story that the purpose of human life is psychological and/or spiritual growth, and that this growth—despite never being clearly defined—inevitably leads to the "actualization of your innate potential" and the manifestation of the "best version" of you.

This is, in fact, a very modern idea. The spiritual traditions of South Asia do not hold this view. They were unanimously oriented toward the goal of discovering the true nature of reality, sometimes known as "enlightenment," though we could simply call it "clear seeing," free of all the mental filters that cause us frustration and misery.

Since the goal of the spiritual life is to see clearly what is already true and always was, the spiritual path requires no growth per se. Clear seeing doesn't require you to be a "better person" or any specific kind of person, other than one genuinely interested in knowing what's true. To put it bluntly, the path to truth-realization is a destructive process, not a constructive one. (Beneficially destructive, of course.) It entails (and necessitates) ridding yourself of whatever is preventing your clear seeing of what is, such as emotional attachment to your perceived identity and to your stories, opinions, and assumptions.

Let's be very clear: trying to be a "better person" in the sense of causing less harm and more benefit to yourself and others is a perfectly laudable and noble goal—it just has no direct relationship with spiritual awakening (for more on this see "Enlightenment," page 201). The whole reason that one works with the moral values and precepts (*yamas* and *niyamas*, as they're called in Yoga) at the beginning of one's Yoga practice is because that work forms beneficial habits and attitudes that are unlikely to be automatically downloaded by the truth-realization that comes later, but also unlikely to be undone by it.

Contrary to what many assume, spiritual awakening does not come with a built-in moral code (morality being, after all, a social construct), nor does it automatically bring about psychological maturity. For this reason, people who want to have a healthy psyche must do psychological work in addition to their spiritual work. Surprisingly few people realize this, despite abundant examples of gurus and teachers who experientially realized essence-nature (the fundamental truth of our collective being) and/or realized the truth of nonduality but never did psychological work on themselves or educated themselves about social issues. Though truth-realization gives one access to a powerful intuitive faculty (on this, see "Listen to Your Heart," page 41) that is a reliable guide for one's own real-life pragmatic decisions, it does not confer any kind of automatic download vis-à-vis moral issues generally.

Contrary to what many assume, spiritual awakening does not come with a built-in moral code . . . nor does it automatically bring about psychological maturity.

"Okay," you might be thinking, "so the project of self-improvement is largely unrelated to the project of spiritual awakening, but it couldn't possibly undermine the awakening process, could it?" Yes, it could. Let me explain.

What exactly is this best version of themselves that people want to be? All too often, it's a socially conditioned figment of their imagination that is seen as preferable to the psyche and personality they have now. We picture ourselves as the character in a movie who overcomes all odds to become highly successful or highly skilled, regardless of how we started. Or, we imagine the possibility that we could, at some point in the future, consistently be as good and kind and loving as we were on our best day ever. Then we call these imagined possibilities our "potential" or our "best self." But you see the problem? If you think this way, you are creating a situation in which you almost constantly fail to live up to how you think you should be, necessitating some version of self-hatred as a result. Ironically, believing that you are not as you should be drains you of the very life-energy that would otherwise allow you to contribute to the world.

A Clever Disguise

So this near enemy—"I'm trying to become a better person" or "I want to be my best self"—can be insidiously harmful if it is a clever disguise worn by your self-hatred, which is frequently the case. I strongly recommend asking yourself why you want to grow and be a "better person." There are two common reasons that people strive to become better: either because they believe that they are not good enough as they are or because they want to contribute to the well-being of their loved ones and enjoy more harmonious relationships. These two motivations for growth are therefore opposite: the first is self-hatred in disguise, and the second is an expression of love. The first focused on the self, and the second is focused on benefitting others. (Nevertheless, it is possible to have both motivations at the same time.) But even the second motive can be a disguise worn by the ego: Do you truly long to contribute to others' well-being, or do you just want them to see you as a "good person"? The latter motive is again self-hatred in disguise because one needs validation from others in direct proportion to the degree of one's self-doubt and sense of unworthiness.

Here is my radical proposition: all attempts at growth motivated by disguised self-hatred ultimately fail and often cause unintended harm. This is because the motive is rooted in a falsehood: that you're somehow inadequate, not good enough, or not who you're supposed to be. Falsehood can never be the basis for authentic and lasting change.*

All attempts at growth motivated by disguised self-hatred ultimately fail and often cause unintended harm.

By contrast, Yoga teaches that in truth, you are already whole and perfectly you, even before you engage in any growth or self-improvement. If it's so, that's a truth that is eminently worth discovering. Can you imagine how liberating it would feel to experience yourself that way?

Growth is natural for a healthy human being, but it doesn't redress some fundamental deficiency. There is no such thing as a fundamental deficiency, despite what our prevailing cultural narrative says. Each person perfectly instantiates the version of personhood that they embody. A tree is a tree at five feet high or at sixty feet high; it doesn't become worthy of being called a tree only at a specific height. It perfectly expresses its tree-ness at any stage of its growth

*Here someone might argue that self-hatred could, in some cases, be the starting point for beneficial change, for example in the case of someone who hits rock bottom with an addiction, is disgusted with themselves and where they have ended up, and resolves to quit. But I would argue that if that person really does make a beneficial and lasting change, it's because they love something they sense within themselves: the potential they possess for living a different sort of life. They sense, on some level, their own innate potential and they act out of love for it, which is love for themselves. If they truly just hate themselves, by contrast, they will believe their negative self-stories and those stories will turn into self-fulfilling prophecies. Someone who truly believes they are a failure blocks their own access to their inner power to make change. One must sense, as David Gray puts it, a "pinprick of light" within oneself as the starting point for lasting beneficial change. Such change is not so much something one *does* as it is something one opens to, nurtures, and allows to unfold.

process. Tat tvam asi, as the ancient Upanishads say—that's how you are as well. You are perfectly human, right now. Your so-called flaws do not indicate unworthiness or deficiency any more than the dark spots on the moon indicate some kind of lunar unworthiness or deficiency. Everyone has flaws, and your unique set of flaws do not uniquely vitiate your value. Flaws are just part of being human. It's how we're supposed to be.

When others express dissatisfaction with your behavior(s), the ego interprets that in terms of a personal failing, but in reality, there's no such thing as a personal failing; there is just the fact of how well or how poorly you conform to someone's moral code, or the moral code of your community of humans. And the ability to conform to moral codes or cultural norms is a function of causes and conditions that you didn't choose (like your genes and upbringing). Now, if others' dissatisfaction with your behavior compels you to change that behavior, there are again two reasons for doing so. If you believe you're not okay as you are and you need to change in such a way as to win others' approval, you might make earnest attempts to change, but you will simultaneously come to resent the people who don't accept you as you are and who place this burden of having to change upon you, and that resentment will inevitably taint your relationships with them.

If, on the other hand, you want to change your behavior out of a loving desire to contribute to others' well-being and your own, because of the intrinsic joy and satisfaction in making such a contribution, your growth will not only be untainted by resentment but also take a course that is beneficial for all involved, including yourself. In the first paradigm, you risk not being true to yourself and sacrificing your integrity to please others. In the second paradigm, you inevitably contribute to others' well-being without being untrue to yourself because your motivation is love, and being untrue is also unloving.

Considering this, it is incumbent upon you to do some self-inquiry: Is your attempt to change any given behavior based in love or self-hatred? Here's a clue: if your striving to change is hard and effortful, if you beat yourself up for perceived failures in that process and need acknowledgement for perceived successes, it's almost definitely based on self-hatred. By contrast, if you feel intrinsically nourished by the process of growth and don't think of it in terms of success and failure, it's almost definitely based on love.

Let's look at the example of someone who has decided to give up alcohol for thirty days because of health considerations. If halfway through their period of abstinence they have a glass of wine after a challenging day, they might subsequently view themselves as a failure. But this is a nonbeneficial view—in fact, if you see such an incident as a failure on your part, that makes it more likely that you will abandon the discipline altogether and lose the benefit. The benefit of renouncing a dependency for thirty days is hardly undone by one act of indulgence; however, it will almost certainly be undone by believing the failure story. Remember, seeing yourself as a failure will prompt actions that confirm that view because the ego would rather be right than happy, every time. Nearly every negative self-image becomes a self-fulfilling prophecy.

The ego would rather be right than happy.

Furthermore, adhering successfully to a prescribed moral code has its own pitfalls. Those who do so tend to be harshly judgmental of those who don't. If you ask the average person who their most judgmental friend is, they will likely name a person who perceives themselves as morally upright (whether that person is a conservative Christian or a vegan yogi).

So do yourself a favor: instead of trying to be a better person based on the narrative of perceived or imagined deficiencies, practice radical self-acceptance first and foremost.* On that firm foun-

*And please note that self-acceptance does not mean self-approval! Approval is just the inverse of disapproval, and acceptance is not part of that judgmental paradigm; it's simply the realization that you couldn't *in this moment* be different from how you are—and how you are in this moment is perfectly okay because it couldn't be otherwise.

dation, you can open up to feedback from others and then, based on that feedback, decide what you're actually inspired to change out of love for yourself and others. And, as part of your self-acceptance, you accept whatever degree of inspiration you have in whatever areas you have it, and you don't imagine it could or should be otherwise.

With this reflection, we begin to see that "my best self" can only be an idealized image of a future possibility that all actualities fall short of. If you believe that this "best self" is what you should be, then you are not loving or accepting yourself as you are now. Such loving acceptance generates the vital energy needed to effect beneficial change in any sphere while the lack thereof drains that vital energy, leaving you enervated.

People who try to change on the basis of self-hatred (disguised or not) either don't change their behaviors for very long or manage to change their behavior but remain as miserable as they were before the change. This is because only a loving relationship with what is can generate the degree of vital energy necessary for lasting beneficial change. Therefore, if you don't yet have thorough self-acceptance, spend the precious life-energy you do have on cultivating it, which increases your sense of aliveness and concomitant inspiration.

Your Intrinsic Value

Consider this proposition: your intrinsic worth is proven by your very existence. Anyone who says otherwise is selling you a story about the kind of person they think you should be. This should not be taken to mean that there's no value in working on yourself; in fact, there's great value in it because it makes possible deeper and more fulfilling human relationships. But whether you've done that work has nothing to do with your intrinsic value. Someone rejecting you or declining to be friends with you doesn't reflect your intrinsic value. Rather, it is simply a function of their conditioning and their preferences. To believe otherwise is another instantiation of the egoic thinking that generates most of your suffering. (The ego, here, constitutes the act of taking things personally or blaming other's choices on oneself (for more on this, see "Ego," page 215).) If you've done the kind of basic psychological work that makes you easier to get along with, you likely have more friends than you otherwise would, but it doesn't make you an intrinsically better person. "Better person" is nothing but a mental construct. In every moment, each human being perfectly instantiates the unique aspect of the One that they embody. It couldn't be otherwise.

In conclusion, if you are investing energy in growth and change out of love for yourself and others and out of the desire to express that love in beneficial ways, then not even a little effort goes to waste, as Krishna says in the Bhagavad Gītā. But if your attempts to change are based in veiled self-hatred, you might cause more harm to yourself and others than if you consciously decided not to change or grow at all, ever. One of the most beneficial things you can do for yourself and others is renounce all attempts to change until you have thorough self-acceptance. The key word there is *attempts*—even without any specific attempts on your part, if you have a contemplative practice, life will grow you naturally, and probably do a better job at it.

If you've done the kind of basic psychological work that makes you easier to get along with, you likely have more friends . . . but it doesn't make you an intrinsically better person.

The truth to which "I want to be my best self" is a near enemy is perhaps this: embodied consciousness, by its very nature, enjoys endlessly reinventing itself and discovering more of itself, and what we call growth is a huge part of that. But this growth doesn't have an end point (such as becoming the imaginary person you think you "should" be); embodied consciousness engages a growth process just because it enjoys growing. The mind loves to create imagined end points, but the point of playing a game is just to enjoy playing it, not to get to the end of it. Growing is, in a sense, a form of playing: an intrinsically rewarding activity and a natural form of expression for a healthy body-mind. In no way does that activity need to contradict the fact that you already are that which you seek.

NEAR ENEMY #4

Be in the Moment

THIS IS PERHAPS THE NEAREST of all the near enemies, in that the practice of presence is indeed central to many spiritual disciplines and in no way antithetical to the spiritual life. However, the injunction to "be in the moment" or "be here now" can easily be misinterpreted in ways that make it a near enemy.

Eckhart Tolle's *The Power of Now* was a hugely successful book—one that I view as the product of an authentic spiritual awakening—and yet its impact on mainstream culture has been, for the most part, incredibly superficial. Nowadays, people who consider themselves spiritual will often say to someone looking at their smartphone, in a disparaging tone, "Hey, why don't you try being present, man?" The other person can obviously respond, "I *am* being present, with my messages, dude . . . bug off!" When applied to others, the injunction to "be present" easily becomes a spiritualized mask for our desires and judgments. What if, instead of spiritual bullying, the first person had articulated a real desire by saying something like "Hey, I'd really like some of your attention; I want to share something with you"?

Many people still believe that being in the present moment means not thinking about the past or future, and this straw man version of the teaching has been rightly criticized by some intellectuals. Avoiding thoughts of the past easily becomes a form of spiritual bypassing* in which we avoid taking responsibility for our actions and making amends. Avoiding any thought of the future may make you downright irresponsible, both personally and sociopolitically. A great German philosopher argued that humans are precisely those creatures who always have their past with them and are always living toward their future, and that it is awareness of mortality that gives human life meaning, an idea that classical Tantra also embraced.**

Avoiding thoughts of the past easily becomes a form of spiritual bypassing in which we avoid taking responsibility for our actions and making amends.

So though one can certainly enter meditative states of total timelessness, there's nothing particularly spiritual about ignoring the past and future in one's everyday life.

You Can't Be Anywhere but Here

As a matter of direct experience, it is of course impossible to *not* be in the present moment. You can't be anywhere but here, and you can't be any*when* but now. If you are lost in thought about past or future, you are lost in thought *here* and *now*. Acknowledging this simple

*For a definition of spiritual bypassing, see upliftconnect.com/spiritual-bypassing.

**The philosopher in question being Martin Heidegger, who certainly *was* a great philosopher, indeed one of the most original and sophisticated thinkers of the twentieth century, notwithstanding the fact that he was also, for a time, a member of the Nazi party. These days it has become fashionable to dismiss someone's entire body of work on the basis of their moral transgressions, but in the case of Heidegger, this is only possible for one who has neither read nor understood his work. His masterpiece *Being and Time*, for example, contains nothing that could be used to justify a fascist ideology.

truth pushes us to inquire more deeply: What does it mean to practice being in the present moment?

We can understand the spiritual injunction to be present in any one of three ways. First and perhaps most importantly, being present means *being attentive to the whole of your experience*. Attentive to your body, your environment, your thoughts, your feelings, your needs, others' needs . . . indeed, the totality of what is present *now* (which can include aspirations for the future or reflections on the past). In this sense, being present is a practice we can engage in for some part of every day, but we cannot engage in it all the time because many tasks call for close focus, a focus in which we release awareness of everything but the task at hand.

Meditation can be simply that: paying attention to the whole of your experience. (Some would argue that if you're paying exclusive attention to one thing, like your breath, that's not meditation but rather concentration, which yields its own distinct benefits.) Why practice this kind of meditation? Because the more we pay attention to the whole of our experience, the more alive we feel, the more embodied we become, the more successfully we connect with others, and the more frequently we notice the subtle signals that life gives us, both the pointers toward wondrous opportunities and the small warning signs that, if heeded, can prevent major shit shows.

When people think of the future, they usually lose themselves in mental images of possible futures, whether blissful or terrible. The problem with being lost in thought about possible futures is twofold. First, humans (including you) are simply terrible at predicting how they will feel in any given circumstance (as abundantly proven by Harvard psychologist Dan Gilbert), so you are wasting your time in trying. Second, by paying attention to those mental images of the future instead of to your whole experience of what's going on now, you become less intimate with what is, and thus less prepared for whatever is yet to come.

Think about it. Whatever is yet to come will necessarily be an organic development of what is already happening now. Therefore, the best way to be prepared for the future is to pay attention to the whole of your experience in the now, especially its subtle dimensions, like the little intuitive feeling that a certain situation is not quite right. (I would suggest that you don't leap to conclusions about such feelings but just track them until they become more specific pointers or signs.) Listening to your whole body is a great way to maintain its health, and listening to your whole heart-mind is crucial for knowing what you really feel and want.* Paying attention to your whole experience is necessary for your nonconceptual intuitive wisdom (pratibhā) to be fully operational.

This brings us to the second version of the practice of "being in the present moment," which I received from the wonderful spiritual teacher Adyashanti, with whom I used to sit retreats: being present, he said, means relaxing the personal will directed toward an imagined future, whether that imagined future is one minute or ten years off. Our ability to appreciate what *is,* is seriously undermined when we're always trying to get somewhere. Here are some examples:

- Instead of connecting with another human being for the sake of connection, we see the connection opportunity as instrumental toward some future end, in which case we inevitably objectify the person in front of us. They become no more real than a video game character.
- Instead of enjoying the miracle of a slow and sensual kiss, we're already anticipating what might come next.
- Instead of engaging all the learning opportunities at our current job, we're just half-assedly "doing time" until our big break.

---

*I use the term heart-mind (corresponding to the Sanskrit word *citta*) to indicate that, contrary to popular belief, our emotional faculty is not at all separate from our mental faculty. For more on this, see my book *Tantra Illuminated.*

- Instead of gratitude for the abundance of blessings that are already here in our life now, we imagine how happy we could be if only . . . (fill in the blank).

Or perhaps your personal will is anxiously directed toward an imagined terrible future, which equally undermines your ability to appreciate what is. When we live with the tension of the personal will directed toward an imagined future, we live in a mind-world maze of possibilities instead of the vivid aliveness of intimacy with what is.

Living this way, we constantly rob from ourselves: we steal away our own happiness, deferring it indefinitely to a tomorrow that never comes. If you place your happiness in the future, that's where it will stay. Relaxing the personal will directed toward an imagined future helps us discover the richness of the *now*. The real arc of progress in life, I argue, is not forward but down—deepening into the total experience of the now.

The third version of the practice of presence is the natural culmination of the first and second versions (when practiced over years). I refer to that extraordinary mode of being in which the three primary centers of embodied consciousness—head, heart, and low belly—are open and clear, free of resistance to whatever energy wants to flow through, and fully connected both to each other and to the world. The majestic wonder and the radiant aliveness of this state is beyond description. When stabilized, it is the culmination of all spiritual, psychological, and somatic development.

So when someone talks about "being in the present moment," ask yourself, What do they really mean? Are they talking about *being attentive to the whole of one's experience*? Or are they suggesting *relaxing the personal will*? Or are they *talking about being fully open, connected, and in harmony with what is*? Or, on the other hand, are they using a spiritual catchphrase to mask their desires and judgments? Or just parroting fashionable spiritual lingo without knowing exactly *what* they mean by it?

Spiritual teachings cannot transform our lives unless we deeply investigate what they really mean—that is, what way of being they are pointing to. If we do not so investigate, any of them can be near enemies to the truth instead of truth.

CONTEMPLATIVE EXERCISE

Opening to Natural Harmony

Get settled and take a few deep breaths. Relax and bring attention to the sensations of the body. Let your attention be curious and open, yet free of the impulse to label. After a while, widen the scope of attention and be with the totality of experience. For this, you must be very relaxed. Let your attention be in soft focus so you can be with everything equally: sensations, sounds, colors, and so on. Relax until all phenomena become one field of energy, as it were. But don't get sleepy, please! After a while, you can move on to part two of this exercise.

First, soften the low belly, and install there a feeling of willingness to be with the whole field of sensation—all the somatic sensations taken together. Then, soften the heart center, and install there a feeling of willingness to be with whatever emotions, thoughts, or feelings arise. Then, open the center in the head by inviting a sense of transparency there, and installing a feeling of willingness to be with whatever sounds, colors, and smells constitute your environment at this moment. Finally, feel the connection of these three centers. Feel them operating in perfect harmony with each other and their environment. This doesn't have to make logical sense. Just feel it, if you can.

NEAR ENEMY #5

Listen to Your Heart

IN POPULAR CULTURE, the mind and the heart are viewed as being in opposition in some fundamental way. The mind is seen as the locus of thought and rationality, and the heart of emotion, passion, desire, and longing. Rationality and emotion are often seen as being irreconcilable, at least in some instances, and so one must choose between the promptings of the head and of the heart. Some form of this idea goes all the way back to Plato—but that doesn't make it right.

Despite the popularity of this idea, it is fundamentally misleading. Reinforcing this false dichotomy leads us away from truth. "Listen to your heart," when the heart is defined in opposition to the head, is a near enemy of the truth.

There can, of course, be real opposition between what you want to do and what you've been told you should do (or any number of similar internal tensions), but mythologizing this into a struggle between heart and head serves no one.

In ancient Indian culture and philosophy, there aren't separate words for *mind* and *heart*. That is, any word that means "mind" in the Sanskrit language also means "heart," and vice versa. In other words, this culture never imagined that the locus of the thought and the locus of emotion could be different or distinct. Both thoughts and emotions were understood as vibrations of *citta*, or the heart-mind, somatically located in the center of the chest (the region around and behind the sternum, to be more precise). In other words, premodern South Asian people didn't experience thoughts happening in their heads as we do; they experienced thoughts and emotions both occurring in the center of the chest. The head was considered a locus of awareness but not of thought. We'll return to this important distinction later; suffice to say that it is mostly cultural conditioning that causes us to experience thoughts and emotions in specific locations. In fact, they have no fixed location.*

Wherever we locate it, the proposition that there is in fact a single locus of both thought and emotion (we could perhaps call it the psyche in English) has considerable implications. Thought and emotion are entirely inseparable. We can still usefully distinguish them by saying that thoughts are vibrations of the heart-mind that have a greater linguistic or rational component, and emotions are vibrations of the heart-mind that are less verbal and have a greater "affective charge"—but they exist on a continuum. Because they exist on a continuum, thoughts or stories that we're scarcely aware of can manifest as strong emotions, and emotions we're scarcely aware of can manifest as strong opinions. This relative lack of awareness of one or the other occurs because most of us have trained ourselves to suppress seemingly undesirable thoughts and feelings, which then show themselves in a different form.

---

*You may say, "But I actually feel thoughts happening in my head and emotions in my heart!" Believe it or not, there's evidence that strongly suggests that that is mostly just deep cultural conditioning. We experience thoughts in our head because we associate them with the brain. In premodern Indonesia, by contrast, people felt both thoughts and emotions in their *liver*! The heart/mind division in Western culture has been traced all the way back to the Hellenistic period, which absorbed vying cardiocentric and cerebrocentric influences. (See the fascinating article "Culture and Language: Looking for the 'Mind' inside the Body" by Sharifian et al., 2008.)

It takes a few minutes (or months) to assimilate all the implications of the idea that thoughts and emotions are always inextricably linked. For one thing, it thoroughly undermines the modern tendency to consistently privilege feeling over thought. Just a few generations ago, people were taught to trust their reason over and against their wayward, irrational emotions. Emotion was seen as an unreliable guide to action, to say the least. Now the tables have turned in popular culture. Feeling is sacrosanct. In television interviews, for example, it seems that no one asks for well-reasoned views anymore: we hear questions like "What's your feeling on that?" and answers like "I really feel that. . ." when what follows might be a feeling, a hunch, or just an opinion that is not well thought out or supported by the facts but that the person won't be obliged to defend because, after all, it is their feeling. And feelings are indisputable, right? Emotion is more important than reason in our popular discourse today, and it's continually validated and dramatized by the media.*

Verbal Memes

The way we use the word *feeling* undercuts our ostensible head-heart divide since its usage often bridges the domains of thought and emotion. How we say we feel about something is often nothing more than an opinion based on our conditioning and backed up by emotional attachment. It's an emotionally charged thought. But thought has, in many such cases, been reduced to the level of regurgitated verbal

*Here, a note on terminology. I'm aware of the work of cognitive scientists, like Antonio Damasio, who strongly distinguish the terms *emotion* and *feeling* (seeing emotion primarily as a social behavior), and the work of others, like Joseph LeDoux, who do not strongly distinguish them. Since there is not yet a generally agreed upon definition of *emotion,* I use the term, as I think most people do, to refer to the subjective experience of that which is denoted by words like *sad, angry, happy, excited,* and so on. The word *feeling* has a broader application: it can refer to any felt emotion and to an inclination, a hunch, and so on.

memes: slogans to which one has become emotionally attached for one reason or another. Many people have all but lost the ability to interrogate these slogans, some of which are the near enemies we explore in this book. When we do bother to interrogate them, we often discover that people using the same phrase don't mean the same thing by it.

So what does it mean when someone says "Listen to your heart"? Does it mean "Do whatever you feel like"? Or does it mean "Get in touch with your emotions"? Or perhaps it means "Find out what you really want." Or perhaps even "Set aside others' opinions and desires for you." It depends on the speaker. The most common false dichotomy that many people subject their decision-making to is this: should I make decisions on the basis of my mind's response to the available facts or decide on the basis of the most dominant emotion in my psyche?

I have suggested that it is only through lack of reflection that we picture ourselves as having two opposing centers, mental and emotional, one of which can be privileged over the other. Here we must acknowledge that for someone who believes this picture of things, it can certainly feel as if it's true. They can feel as if there is a conflict between their head and heart (which I suggest is most often a conflict between the internalized narratives of their upbringing and what they really want). But that cannot be taken as evidence of two opposing centers: when one stops believing this picture of things, it ceases to be true. On the spiritual path, the implications of this are significant indeed.

For example, if we self-reflect on the basis of the hypothesis that the emotional heart and logical mind constitute two ends of a single spectrum, we discover that our emotional states are nearly always linked to a narrative or thought pattern that often lives at the threshold of conscious awareness. The more deeply embedded a narrative is, the less aware we are of it—rather than thinking it as a conscious thought, it becomes a lens through which we see (and feel) reality. For example, if you believe deep down something like "Things almost never go my way," you will tend toward cynicism and depression, noticing every event that could be interpreted as a failure but failing to celebrate those events that could be interpreted as successes. All deeply embedded narratives recur of their own accord as habitual thought patterns happening in the background, scarcely noticed yet still shaping our moods moment to moment. When we are pulled from our natural state of contentment* into a contracted state (a state where we seemingly become a dense mass of conflicted thoughts and/or emotions), it is most often because we are framing our experience in the way that gives rise to that particular contraction, whether we notice it or not. Therefore, disliking any given state (or disliking yourself for being in that state) is missing the mark because the contracted state expresses our natural embodied intelligence by signaling that self-reflection is needed. Every form of discontent invites reflection, and upon such reflection we often discover a mental frame or "story" about our situation that can be discarded or at least given nuance, leading to the release or softening of the contracted state.

What Is Your Story?

When you investigate, being ruthlessly honest and radically sincere with yourself, you will probably find that your "bad day" (or week or month) was sparked by a disempowering or negative thought pattern that you believed and spun into a story, a mental image of yourself or your life—a story that undermined your ability to access your natural joy and freedom: "Now that that deal fell through, I'll

*The practice of meditation reveals that the natural state of most if not all human beings is something like affable contentment or pleasant tranquility or gentle aesthetic rapture, since seemingly all meditators who progress far enough with the practice discover this state, as well as that it can become their default state.

probably never make it in this business" or "Someone's always leaving early—probably no one likes my classes." Nothing can drain us of our life-energy energy faster and more effectively than a negative story that seems convincing to the mind.

This is not to say that all suffering is generated by the mind. Some forms of suffering are based in all-too-real external factors (such as an abusive relationship), but it's important to note those forms of suffering are often exacerbated and/or prolonged by the misaligned stories we have about them (such as "I probably deserve this" or "I attracted this situation to myself, so I'm supposed to stay in it to learn something").

The problem is, we are often not aware of our stories as stories. The more the current story fits in with our generalized picture of reality, or our fears about how things "really are," the less it stands out in our awareness. It must be ferreted out with self-reflection. To put this into practice, ask yourself what you are assuming to be true without even realizing it's an assumption. Once you have an answer to that, you can inquire into whether the facts of the matter necessarily compel you to tell that story. What other story could be told, compatible with the same facts, that is far more empowering and uplifting?

Let's look now at the flip side of this paradigm: thoughts, even thoroughly intellectualized ones, are often linked to hidden emotions. I was trained as an academic, and in the world of academia, we are taught to be "objective." As a result, many academics express their intellectual interests as though they exist in a vacuum, divorced from their feelings, their humanity, and their life history. But nothing exists in a vacuum, and once you get to know an academic or an intellectual (especially in my field, that of religious studies), you discover that their specific intellectual projects are very much linked to their life history, psychology, and emotional landscape. And the same is true of anyone who makes seemingly logical arguments for what they believe in and value. By not acknowledging the underlying forces that affect which point of view we argue for, we are making ourselves less objective by virtue of our lack of transparency.*

Let's look at these two scenarios. If you are a so-called heady person, who seems to be more rational than emotional, you now have a tool in your hands: you understand the interdependence of thoughts and emotions that we have discussed. You can note which opinions and views you hold strongly, if seemingly dispassionately, and trace them to a place in your being where they exist as pure emotion. For example, you may have strong opinions about what constitutes justice or fairness. I'll wager that if you trace these abstract views to the emotional landscape half-hidden in your body, you might discover suppressed anger within yourself about the time(s) when you were wronged. What if you were to seek out that anger, scrutinize it, and unlock its beneficial power? When you do this, you are not moving from one putative center of your being to another (such as from intellectual "mind" to emotional "heart") as much as uncovering the hidden foundations of subtle structures that are larger than you realized.

Feelings Versus Facts

If you're more emotional than rational, you might greatly benefit from learning to compensate for the way in which the emotional charge from unresolved past experiences compels you to hold opinions that might not be true. Remember, just because they feel true doesn't mean they are. If you gently push yourself to admit that what you think you know might merely be a feeling of certainty rather

---

*This is acknowledged to varying degrees in some academic fields. For example, the concept of social location is a way for a scholar to acknowledge where they're coming from and what biases they may hold.

than actual knowledge,* and then open-mindedly consult the actual facts and verifiable evidence (with the support of your clear-minded friends, perhaps), such contemplation may yield palpable benefits in both your life experience and your relations with others.** This teaching should not, of course, be taken to imply that emotional convictions are probably false simply because they are emotional. It simply invites you to investigate deeply to discern the difference, if any, between what you feel is true and what is true regardless of your feeling about it.***

To summarize, thoughts and feelings exist within a single continuum, where the thought end of the spectrum is defined by its wordiness, its rationalization, and partial suppression of the emotional charge underpinning it, and the feeling end is defined by its relative loss of verbalization and appearance of the full charge of the emotion involved. When we discover the emotional underpinning of a thought, or the hidden assumption fueling an emotion or mood, we are bringing into full awareness the totality of a certain pattern of energy in our psyche. Bringing it into full awareness gives

---

*On this, see Robert Burton's rather brilliant book *On Being Certain: Believing You Are Right Even When You're Not* (New York: St. Martin's Press, 2008).

**Here we need the caveat that, at times, reliable evidence is not available to us, or if it is, we may not know how to interpret it, lacking the necessary training. In this case, if we're honest, we must replace our opinion with an admission that whatever we might feel, we simply *don't know*. If a decision must nevertheless be made in the matter, we are better off trusting the most reliable and acknowledged experts in the relevant field, if it's the sort of decision that can be informed by expertise, or trusting the intuitive faculty that reaches much deeper than emotion, if it's not (more on this later in the chapter).

***It's worthwhile to note here that many people feel certain about something that is unsupported by the evidence even when that felt certainty causes them suffering. Fear often plays a significant role in this kind of false certainty. For example, some people feel certain that the world is a more dangerous place than it used to be even though the crime statistics for their part of the world show a marked decline in violent crime. Since the belief in question renders sensical the fear they feel (perhaps generated in the first place by distortive, sensationalistic "news" media), they are convinced the belief is correct, even though it doesn't make them feel good. So our motives for belief are sometimes rooted in making sense of our emotions rather than simply being a matter of what we *want* to be true.

us insight into its nature and its effect on our moment-to-moment experience.

How does a spiritual practitioner who acknowledges heart-mind unity make a decision? If we can't reliably privilege thought over emotion or vice versa, how do we find clarity? On the path of Yoga, a practitioner seeking to make a wise decision is invited to carefully and soberly consult all aspects of their being—taking note of thought, feeling, memory, wordless intuition, and embodied instinct—and balance them all with the input of their teacher(s) and most trusted friends. They do not habitually privilege one source over the others. To do so on a consistent basis, they know, is to move ever further into disintegration.

But you may ask, when it comes to making decisions, is there not a final arbiter, an inner tiebreaker, a place within us where the buck stops, as it were? According to the spiritual tradition of Shaiva Tantra, there is.

That tradition teaches that our essence-nature, the core of our being, which is also the ground of being itself, cannot be grasped by the mind and so it goes by many names (while being ultimately nameless)—in Sanskrit it is called *sāra* ("essence, core"), *madhya* ("center"), *svabhāva* ("true nature"), *ātman* ("real self, soul"), and *śivatva* ("divinity"). It is also sometimes called *hṛdaya*, the sacred heart of being. So, if we ask after the real truth in relation to which "Listen to your heart" is a near enemy, it is, well, "Listen to your Heart"—where "Heart" means the deepest core of your being, the quiet presence beyond both thought and emotion.

The intuitive wisdom that arises from the heart is called pratibhā in Sanskrit.* It's kind of like a quiet pulse of deep inner knowing, or a wordless sensing of which way the current of life wants to take you.

---

*This term, in this specific sense, is peculiar to the literature of Nondual Shaiva Tantra.

It's very difficult to put into words, since it is inherently nonverbal, but I will try to point toward it.

Pratibhā simultaneously means intuitive insight, embodied instinct, and spontaneous inspiration. It is a subtle, nonverbal, nonemotional intuitive faculty that all of us have but few of us get quiet and still enough to sense. Only on rare occasions is it perceptible above the din of the compulsively thinking mind. Pratibhā, unlike the mind, never defends or explains or justifies itself but simply offers itself as a gift. It feels distinctly different from a whim or preference. It's something much deeper. It often feels like an inexplicable magnetic pull, but it's subtly different from an attraction, lacking the anxiety or excitement inherent in the latter. Sometimes it's just a tiny, quiet feeling of "Yes. This." Other times, it feels like a deep current, as powerful as a slow but mighty river, a persistent silent pull toward anything that aligns with both your essence-nature and the greater pattern of life. Following that pull immediately yields a feeling of rightness, though not following it doesn't necessarily feel wrong . . . just less right. (Though sometimes, if the stakes are high enough, acting against pratibhā will feel very, very wrong for some people, even to the point of making one feel ill.) That feeling of rightness might be accompanied by some fear of the unknown because pratibhā often leads us beyond the domain of what we think we know. It's normal to feel apprehensive when following the pull of pratibhā.

CONTEMPLATIVE EXERCISE

Feeling the Pull of Innate Intuition

—

Perhaps you're stuck with a decision about who to date, which job offer to accept, or where to relocate. When you need to make a decision in which the options are already well understood, try this technique. First, practice your favorite meditation technique for a few minutes to become relatively calm and centered. Then select two, three, or four (no more than that) options available to you and mentally place them in space around you—for example, one on either side, one in front, and one behind (if there are four). Take a little time to feel into each option, paying more attention to its vibe than the facts you know about it. Then come back to the center and take a few deep breaths, letting go of any worry about making the "right" decision by affirming that you can trust your inner knowing. Then notice if you feel something like a gentle pull in one direction or another. It might feel like a magnetic pull, or it might feel like a warmth or inner brightening in one direction or another. That's your answer. That's what you can trust. If you want to be very sure, simply repeat the exercise a few days in a row, placing the options in different locations each time (to compensate for possible confounding factors).

Sensing the Pattern

Consistently following this instinctive wisdom, this innate intuition called pratibhā, can make your whole life feel permeated by ease and flow (even though there may be challenges at the same time) because you are in harmony with the greater pattern of which it is an expression. Many spiritual traditions teach that there is a deep structure to existence, a pattern of being if you will, that instantiates on every possible level, from the movements of celestial bodies to the behaviors of insect populations. Only humans have a faculty that second-guesses the pattern or distracts us from it or impedes our ability to follow it: the discursive mind conditioned by our culture and upbringing. Since pratibhā is a kind of compass to sense the natural flow of the pattern, it provides a far sounder basis for action than our narrow, provincial, ephemeral, mostly arbitrary cultural conditioning. The pattern of being naturally moves toward harmony, so following your deepest inner intuition—which is an expression of the pattern—is always the most beneficial course.

This inner wisdom inclines in one direction or another for the benefit of all beings, which is one key way it is different from the desires of the heart-mind, which usually tend to move toward what is beneficial for you personally. So, the inner wisdom won't necessarily lead you toward what you most like or enjoy. (However, through spiritual practice, for some rare individuals the heart-mind can become fully aligned with the inner wisdom; in Sanskrit terms, citta becomes yoked to pratibhā. Then you want what life wants.) Another way to distinguish them is that the desires of heart-mind are mercurial and protean, while pratibhā is steady, slow, and inexorable (e.g., inexorably pulling you toward or away from a particular person in your life, or toward or away from a particular career path). Heart-mind expresses as endless thoughts like "Maybe I should do A, or maybe I should do B—but also, I want to make sure I have C." In contrast, pratibhā is a wordless undercurrent, the mysterious silent pull toward the heart's deepest longing—and it's there even before you consciously know what you truly long for.

I have said that a spiritual practitioner seeking to make a wise decision will consult all aspects of their being and not consistently privilege one over all the others. But after sufficient spiritual practice, when you have clear access to pratibhā, it's natural and right to make it the final arbiter. One still needs to consult the various aspects of one's being, since this fleshes out the landscape within which pratibhā moves. Appointing her (the Sanskrit noun is feminine) queen of the landscape of selfhood creates a life experience of harmony because all internal disagreements are automatically resolved by the deep inner knowing that is neither a thought nor a feeling nor an impulse. In this way, all the faculties of the heart-mind come into orbit around pratibhā, the wordless wisdom of your innermost being, and it leans toward whichever presented possibility is most deeply aligned with the overarching pattern.

The fundamental issue, then, is this: when people hear "Listen to your heart," they often fail to make the relevant and necessary distinction between the emotionally charged beliefs of the heart-mind and the quiet, calm, wordless knowing of their deepest being. The failure to make this key distinction, is, of course, understandable because none of us were taught this in school, and without a contemplative and/or meditative life, one can't reliably access that inner knowing we call pratibhā. If you can't get quiet inside, you can't feel that innate intuitive faculty clearly enough to distinguish it from the shifting tides of emotion and desire. This is why we need meditation.

If this concept doesn't yet resonate for you, I suggest you come back to this teaching later, perhaps after reading the rest of the book. It might, at some point, become surprisingly resonant with your experience. For now, you could set it aside. There's plenty more skeptical myth-busting for you to enjoy and contemplate in the pages ahead.

NEAR ENEMY #6

Love Yourself

SURELY, ONE MIGHT THINK, there is no more unproblematic injunction in the self-help industry and in popular spiritual culture than "Love yourself." Well, think again. When people try to heed this seemingly salutary command, it can lead them into a whole mess of trouble. I'll first describe some of those issues, then I'll try to point toward the truth to which "Love yourself" is a near enemy to the extent that I've been able to discern and experience that truth.

First, what does it mean to love yourself? Therein lies the problem. To perform (or even attempt to perform) this action, one must be internally divided: there must be one part of you doing the loving and another part of you being loved. There is of course nothing wrong with this per se—for example, it may feel downright wonderful to love your inner child after judging or suppressing them for so long.* But however good it feels, and however much psychic relief it

*From the point of view of Yoga psychology, the modern term *inner child* can be taken to refer to an interconnected set of *saṃskāras*, or undigested experiences from childhood or adolescence. When one or more of these saṃskāras get activated (or triggered) by present-day events that exhibit some (even slight) similarity to those past experiences, it can cause a kind of regression in which one's psyche momentarily provides, it's only a short-term solution. Because what it also does is reinforce internal division, and such division does not permit us to experience our natural wholeness.

In Western societies, the influence of the Freudian model of the tripartite self (indirectly based on the Platonic version of the same) is pervasive, and it has set us at war with ourselves: our superego, or conscience, attempts to control the other unruly parts of ourselves, the selfish ego and the impulsive id.* Only in the context of this culturally fabricated inner struggle does the reconciliation offered by the injunction "Love yourself" seem necessary. By contrast, the nondual tradition of Shaiva Tantra offers a sustainable model of internal harmony: the undivided self. According to this view, we are not inherently and irreconcilably partitioned: in truth, we are a single mass of self-aware consciousness that includes many activities within itself, just as the ocean contains many currents but is ever undivided. We'll explore the practical implications of this view toward the end of this section.

First, let's get clear on the issue at hand. The injunction to love yourself reinforces a sense of internal division by being normative: you *should* love yourself, so you will have to continue maintaining this internal division to comply with that mandate. You will have to maintain one aspect of your psyche in an infantile state, needy of love, and keep it separate from another aspect that is doing the loving, an aspect implicitly seen as superior or wiser or somehow more you. But the natural consummation of love, which is melting together or harmonious integration, must be prevented to continue to obey the injunction to love yourself. What a strange paradox!

---

returns to a childlike state and experiences things as the child did, specifically at the age when the as-yet-undigested experience currently being triggered occurred.

*For the sake of simplicity, I am of course oversimplifying the Freudian model here. Also note that the terms *id, ego,* and *superego* derive from Freud's English translator—Freud himself used the terms *the It, the I,* and *the Over-I* (das Über-Ich). His theory of a tripartite psyche was indirectly based on Plato's theory of the tripartite psyche (a word that primarily meant, in Plato's time, "self" or "soul"), which has influenced Western culture for more than two thousand years.

On the social level, we can hardly ignore the fact that the injunction "Love yourself" has also bolstered an increasing trend toward narcissistic attitudes in our society. This is in part because, just as we implicitly believe others need to behave a certain way to merit our love, most of us subconsciously believe that we need to be special to merit the love we are supposed to have for ourselves. In this way, the belief that we are worthy of love becomes conflated with the need to believe that we are special, that we are a cut above the rest in some way. But this need to believe that you are special has a dark side because it requires that you look down on most other people, considering them to be merely ordinary.

Now you may think that you already do love yourself. But does that mean that you merely have approving thoughts about yourself? I once had a student who claimed to love herself and yet was terribly unhappy being on her own (both in the sense of being single and of being physically alone). I came to realize that this kind of self-love meant that she was committed to the story of her own specialness and lovability, which then created a very painful cognitive dissonance: "I'm so special and lovable, I know I am, so why doesn't anyone love me?" (Where "love me" really means "want me as a life partner"—a common but insidious distortion of the word *love.*)

The Self-Image Machine

All too often we "love" ourselves on the basis of a story of our own specialness or uniqueness. We could call this the Facebook version of love, in which the word simply means "like a lot" and/or "strongly approve of." The great significance our culture places on individual difference is spiritually problematic because, on the spiritual path, we're seeking to realize that which is universal within us and unites us to all other beings. Difference is that which divides us from others, reinforcing the self-image machine we call ego. Moreover, this emphasis on difference points us away from the more basic truths of our existence—because in reality, what we share in common is far more fundamental than what makes us unique (for example, we all have the same biology, the same basic feelings and needs, etc.). Therefore, the cultural emphasis on difference and uniqueness focuses attention on the superficial more than the fundamental and inflates the significance of the former at the expense of the latter.

This need to feel special is even more insidious than we realize. It has contributed to social and cultural divisiveness because it causes us to focus on our subgroup identity more than the needs of the wider society that we are a part of and that we depend on (think of the political divide that has poisoned politics and public schools in the United States). Furthermore, the need to be special has strengthened our emotional attachment to the supposed rightness of our opinions and thus amplified our argumentative nature, and it has corrupted our interpersonal relationships with the mostly fabricated need for constant validation. Last, it has undermined our capacity for empathy since empathy is a kind of human connection that is impossible without the implicit assumption that the other person's feelings and needs are—at least for that moment—just as valid and worthy of attention as one's own.

The need to feel special even undermines one's self-love because, in this paradigm, every time others don't acknowledge your specialness it fosters insecurity, self-doubt, and even self-hatred. Do you know anyone who simultaneously thinks they're so very special and yet is also plagued by insecurity? Of course you do. You may even be that person yourself. If so, there's no shame in it. This is the psychological epidemic of our time. And it's not getting better.

These days, some argue that in a relationship it's healthy to prioritize one's own needs over those of the other while others argue that love means caring about the other person more than yourself. Both views are wrong, I would argue, since a relationship (of any kind) only flourishes when it is regarded as a third entity, prompting both parties to ask not only "What do I need?" and "What do you need?" but also "What does the relationship need?" All three questions need attention for relational harmony to flourish. That's so important that it bears repeating: all three questions need attention for relational harmony to flourish.

The cultural mythos around the specialness of the individual self causes divisiveness on both small and large scales. Let's think for a moment about the large scale, that is, the social scale. "Love yourself" is all-too-often interpreted to mean "Love your identity," which for young people often means *constructing* an identity to love. This identity is often constructed based on markers of difference—sexual difference, racial/ethnic difference, political difference, and so on. The tragedy is that this can create needless suffering. Today we're witnessing culture wars based on these differences, even though as human beings we all share much more in common than we don't. When young people learn to focus more on what makes them different from their peers, it exacerbates their suffering.

For example, some young people of color are taught to identify themselves as members of an oppressed class and thereby end up taking on the suffering of Black people in white-majority societies throughout history. If this identification with ethnicity inspires someone to help wipe out the systemic racism that persists in many white-majority societies, we can see some benefit in it that partially compensates for the psychological suffering such identification brings. But I do not sympathize with the view that someone *should* take this path simply because of the color of their skin. Each individual has the right to choose whether to identify with their ethnicity over and above any other aspect of their being (such as, say, their artistic temperament, their talent for math, or their love of athletics). That is to say, the cultural pressure to strongly identify with markers of difference is neither necessary nor salutary. (In this regard, it might be helpful to note that the concept of race has little-to-no scientific basis.)* We must admit that race, the gender binary, the dichotomy of straight versus queer, the dichotomy of liberal versus conservative, and all such divisions are cultural constructs, not facts given to us by nature. Participating in these constructs should be an individual choice. Ideally, that choice would be informed by an awareness of their constructedness—that is, an awareness that reality is far more fluid than any of these mental categories.

Cultural Constructs

Of course, if we acknowledge that race is a cultural construct, we must in the same breath acknowledge that it is a cultural construct that is reified by most of Western society and its institutions, and that reification has very real consequences. Anyone who has experienced being seen in terms of their putative race first and in terms of their humanity second finds that experience dehumanizing and painful. And that pain will not resolve itself without being faced squarely. Facing it necessarily entails accepting the fact that most people believe in the constructed category of race and therefore necessarily view people in terms of it. (And of course, a person's identity as a woman is also culturally constructed by generations of gender normativity; the fact that most people still conflate biological sex and gender indicates how poorly understood its constructedness is.)** We must also acknowledge that a shared experience of oppression or marginalization can create a strong bond among those who identify

---

*See, for example, www.nytimes.com/2017/10/12/science/skin-color-race.html.

**To be clear, I do not hold the view that there is no intrinsic connection whatsoever between biological sex and the cultural category of gender; I am merely saying that they constitute two distinct categories of thought, one biological and the other cultural, with some real though tenuous links between them.

themselves in any of these ways. A young black woman may feel solidarity with others who have suffered the effects of racism even if her own experience of it is minimal, and there's certainly no reason she shouldn't feel that solidarity. But she may come to believe that she herself is oppressed or marginalized based on an ideology she is embracing rather than on the basis of her direct experience. This gives rise to needless suffering. And if that suffering is indeed due to her ideological commitment and her story about herself rather than due to any actual oppression or discrimination in her given case, then it is not intrinsically different from the imagined suffering that white nationalists who believe in the "white replacement" conspiracy theory impute to themselves. This may seem a tendentious statement, but I'm simply trying to point out that identification with any ethnic group can give rise to psychological suffering, whether real, imagined, or both in any given case. The fear and/or hatred and/or sense of victimization that such identification commonly entails is intrinsically the same for all who experience it, and so ironically it is a shared experience with those one regards as "other." People like to believe that their pain, and that of their social group, is somehow unique in quality and/or in degree, but this belief is both false and divisive. For humans, group identity easily shades into tribalism, and tribalism is an artificial division within our shared humanity.

Why does tribalism, here defined as believing in a group identity strongly enough to generate a feeling of opposition to other groups, always cause suffering? There are many reasons, and I'll touch on the two I see as most salient. First, most humans are unable to understand this simple fact: knowing that X is true about a given demographic group on average tells you nothing about an individual member of that group. The fact that people of color have historically been marginalized in countless ways is no guarantee that the person of color standing in front of you today has been the victim of such marginalization. And likewise, the fact that white people have historically been privileged over and against others in US society purely because of their perceived ethnicity* does not necessarily mean that a random white person standing in front of you today has been able to leverage any of that historical privilege. To believe otherwise is to sacrifice truth on the altar of currently fashionable discourse. Here, of course, we're not getting into probabilities, and probabilities are important: a person of color in a white-dominant society is very likely to have confronted some form of racism, and that a person perceived as white in that society is likely to have benefitted from some form of white privilege. I'm merely saying that one cannot assume either in an individual case. Yet such assumptions are rife in the context of tribalism, obscuring the unique humanity of the given individual. Though we all share the same feelings and human needs, each individual's experience is unique and unpredictable. This is the beautiful paradox of being human.

Second, for many people, trying to love one's identity entails seeing it in opposition to the perceived identity of others—others who then easily become objectified. There's nothing inherently wrong with creating and celebrating group identity. But if our hypothetical young black woman, justifiably angered by the countless crimes of the white men of history who have sought to preserve and extend their unearned privileges at the expense of Black and/or indigenous people of color, sees a white man standing in front of her today as a representative of those crimes instead of an individual human of as-yet unknown values and experiences, is she not committing the same sin of objectification on the basis of race that has been so incredibly painful for members of her own group?

Some of you reading this right now are upset that this topic has been broached at all in a book that is supposed to be about spiritual philosophy, and you're wondering if personal agendas of the author

---

*"Perceived ethnicity" is a valid phrase here, as anyone who has studied the history of Italian and Irish immigrants in America—who for a long time were *not* considered white—is well aware.

are encroaching where they don't belong. But the issues of identity, its constructedness, and the obstacle it poses to truth-realization are and always have been of central concern to the South Asian spiritual traditions on which this book is based. Spiritual awakening in these traditions necessarily includes and entails waking up from all culturally constructed forms of identity, including caste, gender, and race.

Still, I must acknowledge that, of course, it is problematic for one inhabiting a body perceived as white and male to write about the experiences of cultural minorities. But the point I'm trying to make is not at all related to any specific identity: it relates to the potentially dire, unforeseen consequences of viewing self-love as necessarily including love of one's identity, which runs the risk of failing to see the constructedness of identity and taking on the pain of the entire social group with which one identifies.

I also need to make clear here that calling identity a cultural construct does not in any way constitute a belittlement of the enormous pain experienced by members of social groups that have been subject to systemic oppression and marginalization. The argument here rather, seeks to acknowledge that their oppression is partially due to the inability of culture to see that its categories are constructed. When humans believe that their ideas about gender and race are based on biology rather than cultural constructs, that is to say thoughts about gender and race, then oppression or marginalization is certain to result.

To sum up the problem of identity from the spiritual perspective: you unnecessarily amplify your suffering if you believe "I suffer because of being a woman; I suffer because of what I am" instead of "I suffer because some people view me in terms of my gender first and in terms of my humanity second (or not at all), and because those people have deeply entrenched prejudices about my gender." The principle likewise applies to race or any other identity construct.*

*And the issue called intersectionality is all too real because if a woman is sometimes seen in terms of her gender first and her humanity second, a black woman is

The solution to this problem is, of course, to see every single person as a human first and foremost. A human with the same basic feelings and needs as anyone else. This does not suggest that it's okay to subsequently fail to acknowledge that person's group identity (if they claim one) and the suffering they might have endured based on belonging to that group.

In nondual spirituality, seeing someone's humanity also entails seeing their divinity—that is, seeing them as an intrinsically whole and complete expression of the One. If you truly see their humanity, you see their intrinsic equality to all other humans, and if you see their concomitant divinity, you see that they are perfect as they are right now.

Everything I've said here is consonant with Yoga philosophy because it, depending on the school of thought, says "You are not your body, you are pure spirit, which is neither white nor black nor male nor female" (the view of so-called classical Yoga) or "You are consciousness, and consciousness is everything, so you are your body, but no more than you are the earth and sky, the sun and the rain, and all other bodies too" (the view of nondual Shaiva Tantra). Either way, according to this view, even though your suffering might be partially contingent how others perceive your body, your pain is *not* a uniquely female kind of pain or a uniquely black kind of pain or a uniquely queer kind of pain. It is a human kind of pain. When you feel it, you are having an experience that you share with virtually all other humans—the pain of having others confuse your selfhood with your body. Everyone has been objectified at one point or another, and objectification is a failure to see your beingness, and that is nearly always painful or frightening. Failure to see the truth

---

sometimes seen in terms of her humanity *third*, and a queer black woman is sometimes seen in terms of her humanity *fourth*, and so on.

of being, in this view, is the direct or indirect cause of virtually all human suffering.*

The teachings of Yoga philosophy encourage us to release identification with the body and the mind, but they also encourage us to hold compassionate space for the pain suffered by any given body-mind, including your own. In that space of loving awareness, the pain can resolve. Furthermore, the choice to affiliate oneself with a particular social group and champion its rights as a member thereof is not irreconcilable with Yoga philosophy, as some people seem to think, since you do not have to believe that you are the body-mind to honor it, care for it, and advocate for its rights in society.

True Self Love

So what is the spiritual truth to which "Love yourself" is a near enemy? It's ever so hard to put into words, but it's very much worth the attempt. It has nothing in particular to do with loving your inner child, believing that you're special, or valorizing your cultural identity. It's something much softer and subtler than that, and ultimately much more potent.

It entails no longer rejecting or denying any part of yourself, any emotion or impulse or feeling or memory, until your self-acceptance becomes so complete and profound that these various currents of your being cease to be seen as separable parts and become integrated with the central self. Everything in the internal landscape of experience is fully allowed—even welcomed. Not approved, not identified with, but fully and lovingly allowed to be as it is. Every current of experience is allowed to move through the body-mind field, and as a result, the central self becomes amplified by the merging of all

*Here I'm not distinguishing the terms *pain* and *suffering*, though in other contexts such a distinction might be pedagogically useful.

these previously exiled and rejected parts, until the central self has become the whole self, the entirety, and one experiences oneself as a seamless unity: thoroughly undivided. All the stories around pain, sadness, happiness, and discomfort fall away in light of the desire to become intimate with one's life-energy in its countless different forms. Blaming others and oneself falls away, the impulse to construct a self-image based on emotional experiences falls away, and the breath moves more deeply and freely. No aspect of experience is resisted or denied: everything is allowed to be and allowed to move through. This is true self-love.

Then, little by little, more and more, a profound gratitude for one's existence begins to dawn. A reverence for the very fact of being itself. Then one discovers that *love* is not really a transitive verb, requiring an object; that it's not about loving yourself after all but rather about discovering that on the deepest level of being, *you are love,* and the love that you are manifests as total acceptance of all that arises in your inner experience. Given enough time, this acceptance naturally results in integration and wholeness.

This is something far beyond self-esteem or self-approval. This love eventually transcends self altogether and overflows into profound love for the whole of existence: being itself.

In fact, that's how you can determine whether you do have real self-love: Does this cherishing of the miracle of your own precious existence spill over into gradually increasing reverence for all beings?

If not, maybe it's still just a mental construct of self-love, such as self-approval or self-praise—at best a near enemy of the truth.

May each of us realize that our worth is proven by our very existence and that no further proof is necessary. May we see that what we all share far outweighs what we don't. May we see each other as human first and foremost, and may we allow—and celebrate—the natural flow of love and compassion that arises as a result!

CONTEMPLATIVE EXERCISE

Your Innate Value

—

Get settled and take a few deep breaths. Relax as much as possible. Turn your attention to your body—that is, your direct experience of the body in the form of pure sensation. Just be with all the sensations that you collectively call "body." If this triggers any thoughts, gently lay them aside and continue being present with the body sensations, just as they are. (Pause.) Then notice your beingness itself—the simple feeling of being you, prior to any thoughts about yourself. This feeling of being you has always been there, and has always been the same, since you were a child. Fully inhabit this simple feeling of being you, this sense of your own existence. Notice that there is an inherent sweetness in it. A soft, simple, sweet innocence, we could say, though words don't capture it. In your natural presence, you begin to sense your innate value. Only in your natural presence can your innate value be revealed. It can't be proven; it must be sensed directly. What you are is pure presence; it is infinite value. It exists perfectly. Prior to all thought, you already exist perfectly. Relax into this realization.

NEAR ENEMY #7

Everything Happens for a Reason

OF COURSE, AS A LITERAL STATEMENT, "Everything happens for a reason" is true. Everything arises from specific causes and conditions. However, when referring to a challenging or painful event, people use the phrase "Everything happens for a reason" to mean something like "It's all part of God's plan" or "There's an unseen deeper purpose to this event that renders it meaningful, even though you don't know what that purpose is." These ideas are potentially problematic because they are often articulated in a fashion that supports spiritual bypassing, wishful thinking, avoidance of challenging yet worthwhile contemplations, or all of the above.

When the cause of a challenging event is posited as invisible or inaccessible (by assigning it to God or an indiscernible plan instead of human interactions and human fallibility), that can discourage us from soberly investigating the part we played in bringing about that event. This is *spiritual bypassing*: using spiritual clichés to avoid doing difficult emotional labor, despite the great benefits of that labor. As the man who coined the term, John Welwood, defines it, spiritual bypassing is when we "use spiritual ideas and practices to sidestep or avoid facing unresolved emotional issues, psychological wounds, and unfinished developmental tasks. . . . trying to rise above the raw and messy side of our humanness before we have fully faced and made peace with it."*

"Everything happens for a reason" can also be used with the meaning of "The universe is trying to tell you something." ("The universe" somehow being the acceptable stand-in for "God" in many spiritual communities today.) This near enemy can be a temporary ally because it at least encourages some reflection: What am I being told? Is this car accident telling me that it's not safe to text and drive? (Answer: yes.) And of course, there are subtler versions of such inquiry. But this line of thought is also problematic because imagining that God or the divine intelligence of the universe is sending you a message or teaching you a lesson reinforces a false duality between you and "the universe." In the same way, when you use the language of "my higher self," you separate yourself from this imagined angelic version of yourself and reinforce internal division.

Furthermore, believing that the universe sends you messages can get you stuck in a childish or adolescent mindset in which you're trying to learn the right lessons, be a good kid, and toe the universe's line so you will be rewarded with exclusively good karma or perfect harmony with everything. Much more beneficial than this dualistic and misaligned view is the simple recognition that actions have consequences and that when you pay attention to those consequences when they are still minor, they don't get a chance to snowball into something major. When we ignore an opportunity to learn something about the way the world works, that opportunity tends to re-present itself with greater and greater emphasis until we recognize and reflect on it. This does seem to be a feature built into the pattern of things.

---

*From Tina Fossella's interview with John Welwood ("Human Nature, Buddha Nature") in the Spring 2011 issue of *Tricycle: The Buddhist Review*.

So, what is the actual truth to which "Everything happens for a reason" is a near enemy? A phrase that gets closer to the underlying truth is perhaps this one: "This event, like all events, is part of a deeper pattern that expresses the intrinsic intelligence of life-energy, an intelligence that is worthy of your trust." But this phrase, too, is potentially misleading in important ways. I would argue that there is a fundamental pattern to existence—deep structures, symmetries, rhythms, and leitmotifs that encompass all things—even though some aspects of the pattern are far too subtle and complex for us to predict or even describe. In the Western tradition (especially in the teachings of the Stoics), this idea of a single universal complex pattern of existence was called *lógos*,* and in Sanskrit it goes by the name *parā vāk*—the supreme word, where *word* means something like "deep structure" or "underlying pattern" (note that lógos is translated in the Gospel of John as "the Word" as well).

Believing that the universe sends you messages can get you stuck in a childish or adolescent mindset.

I'm not arguing that you "should" unquestioningly trust the pattern because then you're likely still implicitly deferring authority to a "higher power" and exempting yourself from the spiritual work. It's much more beneficial, in my experience, to learn to go beyond your own mind and your mental filters by means of meditation and awareness cultivation, so that you can begin to directly *sense* the pattern. Though we can never understand it with our minds, the feeling of sensing the pattern of existence, which we might call the innate intelligence of reality, is a wondrous and indescribable thing. Once you've sensed it, the next step is to trust it. Trusting the pattern connotes

*"For the Stoics, the logos was the active reason pervading and animating the Universe. It was conceived as material and is usually identified with God or Nature. The Stoics also referred to the seminal logos ("logos spermatikos"), or the law of generation in the Universe, which was the principle of the active reason working in inanimate matter. Humans, too, each possess a portion of the divine logos." A. Tripolitis, *Religions of the Hellenistic-Roman Age* (Grand Rapids: Eerdmans Publishing Company, 2002), 37–38.

a loving surrender to the natural unfolding of life. This is possible when you know in your bones that there is an innate intelligence to life, that nothing can actually go wrong in the natural unfolding of life (though of course we find some threads in the pattern exquisitely painful). Experientially speaking, there's a huge difference between *believing* there's a deeper pattern and actually *sensing* it, and sensing something of its character (as Walt Whitman did when he wrote in "Song of Myself," "a kelson of the creation is love").* And yes, I am saying that it's possible to sense the innate intelligence of the pattern directly, without concept or belief, the same way you see that grass is green.

Is this deeper pattern intrinsically meaningful? Well, yes and no. Conceptually, it's not meaningful at all because it has no message that can be spoken in words and it's not trying to accomplish anything. But nonconceptually, I would say, it's incredibly meaningful in the same way that a flower or a galaxy is meaningful. It means what it is, and what it *is* is beautiful. So, when you come to directly sense the pattern, you sense its ineffable, awe-inspiring beauty, which is somehow all inclusive and all subsuming. After even a mere glimpse of the pattern, you find you can trust it. You trust the natural unfolding of your life, even if you don't understand it. You trust that the universe (as it were) knows exactly what it's doing, and you also see how absurd it is not to trust. And then you probably laugh at yourself like a crazy person.

The ultimate teaching on this subject in classical Tantra is this: yes, everything happens for a reason—and that reason is "everything else that has ever happened." The cause of anything is everything. This is literally true because everything arises from causes and conditions that themselves have causes and conditions, and when you trace it back all the way, everything gets completely entangled and eventually you arrive at the singularity, usually referred to as

---

*A kelson is a beam running the length of a wooden ship and supporting the whole structure; it's the upper part of the keel.

the Big Bang. (That's why Carl Sagan said, on his television show *Cosmos*, "If you wish to make an apple pie from scratch, you must first invent the universe.") So *everything* is the cause of everything. Including retroactively—meaning that both the past and the future are equally causing what you experience as the present, and the present is likewise causing both past and future. (But that's a discussion for another time.) That's how interconnected reality is. That's why classical Tantra teaches that each thing is contained in all things, and all things are contained in each thing—thus, to contemplate any one thing fully is to contemplate everything.* Such is the nature of the pattern.

*Paraphrased from *The Vision of Shiva* (*Śiva-dṛṣṭi*) by Somānanda, chapter 5. This work has been translated by John Nemec.

NEAR ENEMY #8

Everything Happens for the Best

THIS NEAR ENEMY IS, in some ways, a variation on the previous one, but there are considerably different implications to tease out of the truth to which it is adjacent. "Everything happens for the best" is a platitude that religious people tend to offer as a misguided attempt to comfort someone who is going through a painful time. It amounts to "You'll see, some good will come of this painful or challenging event." In the twenty-first century, the proposition that everything happens for the best seems to most people manifestly absurd, so why am I calling this a near enemy, which is a teaching that is *close* to the truth?

Let's begin by comparing this near enemy to a teaching found in an ancient text of classical Tantra: *nāśivaṃ vidyate kvacit,** which means both "Nothing exists that is not God" and "Nothing exists that is not a blessing" because the word *śiva* literally means "blessing" as

**Svacchanda-tantra* chapter 4, verse 314.

well as being a proper name for the Divine (note that unlike English, Sanskrit has no capital letters, allowing for the ambiguity of meaning here). But this phrase must be understood as a kind of verbal shorthand. Even though in the nondual view everything is God, or Divine Consciousness, that obviously does *not* mean to suggest that we experience every single thing (or feeling or thought) as God. Such an experience of all-inclusive divinity (or all-inclusive consciousness) is the result of a radical shift sometimes called spiritual awakening or enlightenment (see "Enlightenment," page 201). By the same token, though anything *can* be experienced as a blessing, we often can't experience it as such without deep spiritual work, especially if it's a painful event.

I like to put it this way: all events contain potential gifts and blessings, and the more intense or challenging the event, the more potential blessing energy it contains. The events we call painful or challenging are, from the spiritual perspective, more accurately called "events that require work to extract their blessing energy." Imagine if you were able to see all painful or challenging events in this way. Wouldn't it be an incredible paradigm shift to experience all challenging events as neither bad nor wrong but simply events that require some work to extract their blessing energy? Note the word *experience* here is carefully chosen: it's usually not enough to simply *see* a blessing in a painful event because that is often nothing but a conceptual overlay, a form of mental self-soothing. There's nothing wrong with that, but we must do deeper inner work if we want to experience the palpable felt-sense *and* clear perception that the painful event is in fact a blessing.

If, in lieu of doing this work, we simply comfort ourselves with belief in the statement "Everything happens for the best," we can feel a little better about things, but in the long run, that very feeling constitutes an obstacle on the spiritual path. When we feel our pain fully without sugarcoating it, we are much more likely to do deeply beneficial inner work.

How do you do this inner work? That depends on the person and on the event in question, but my general guideline is this: first, feel all the emotions triggered by the event fully, pushing none of them away, while at the same time taking care to lay aside the associated stories or mental constructs that attempt to explain why you're feeling these emotions. Allow the emotions to surge through you like a rushing river of energy—or drip through you like a dribbling stream, sink through you like a stone moving through mud, or whatever's authentically happening. Be intimate with the emotional energy, without making a self-image out of it. When it has finished moving through (at least, for the time being), feel into the center, the still point at the innermost core of your being, and let yourself rest in that stillness for a bit. Then you can ask the inner wisdom to reveal the blessing(s) or the gift(s) in this challenging circumstance. Be careful not to jump to a comforting thought or platitude that may or may not be true in this case; feel your way, carefully and honestly, organically and vulnerably, into what your innate wisdom reveals to you—patiently waiting as you would for the slow opening of a beautiful rose.

Authentic Gratitude

How do you know when you have successfully done this work? When you feel authentic *gratitude* for the challenging event. More precisely, you have finished extracting the blessing energy from it when (a) the pain of it is mostly or entirely digested and resolved, and (b) you feel deep gratitude for the event, perhaps even gratitude of the kind that makes your heart overflow and tears come to your eyes. For example, the breakup of a relationship is a painful experience for most people, so much so that they often miss the opportunity to contemplate what they learned from it. Additionally, they may simply numb the pain of the breakup in various ways rather than extract its blessings. How might pain itself be a blessing? Sometimes it can catalyze a spiritual awakening, such as when the person in pain realizes they don't want a happiness that is dependent on another person's behavior but rather long to discover the source of joy within themselves. Such longing is a common catalyst for awakening.

So, the truth in relation to which "Everything happens for the best" is a near enemy is "Everything can happen for the best—if you're willing to do your work." This is why one of my teachers always used to say, about virtually anything, "Let it be for a blessing." He understood that *whatever* it is, it can be a blessing, but that depends on you.

If (and only if) someone managed to extract the blessings from *every* painful or challenging event in their lives, then in reference to *that* person's life, we could rightly say "Everything happens for the best." But we need not aspire to that impossible ideal to deeply benefit from this teaching, which I would summarize like this: *Anything* can be for the best—so do what is necessary to let it be for a blessing.

Everything can happen for the best—if you're willing to do your work.

There are many examples that this is possible even in extreme circumstances. Viktor Frankl experienced his time in a Nazi concentration camp as a blessing in the sense that he found that his affirmation of the value of life was much more powerful, meaningful, and fulfilling than if he hadn't been in a concentration camp.* Christopher Reeve, who once played Superman in the movies, was paralyzed from the neck down, a condition he came to characterize as a blessing for which he was profoundly grateful because it made him develop compassion and devote himself to the rewarding work of helping others. This and many more examples are collected in Dan Gilbert's brilliant book *Stumbling on Happiness*. And it's good to cite extreme examples because they make us think, "If those guys

*The original German title of his book (which became famous under the English title *Man's Search for Meaning*) translated as *Saying "Yes" to Life in Spite of Everything*.

can experience much more challenging conditions than those in my life as a blessing, maybe I can do it too!" That affirmation is valuable as motivation even if you can't know for sure that it's true.

However, I would be remiss not to acknowledge that sometimes, despite their best efforts, a person simply does not have the emotional or spiritual resources to digest the pain and extract the blessing energy of a challenging event. And if they do not, it would be wrong of them to then beat themselves up for it. After all, no one can choose the degree of access they have to their own emotional or spiritual resources in any given moment (see "You Can Choose How to Respond," page 101). No one ever said this work is easy; the question is, Is the effort worth it in every case? The answer, I believe, is yes. Because even if you can't fully digest your experience, there is palpable benefit in even partially doing so.

What is the culmination of this work? How far can a person go with it? Further than you might think. I know of one fully awakened being, someone who likes to refers to himself, using Layman Páng's words, as "an ordinary fellow who's completed his work," who has reached a point where he *effortlessly* experiences every painful and challenging event as a blessing. He trusts the pattern of life (a.k.a. divine intelligence) so deeply that he feels the blessing energy of a painful event *while in the midst of the pain,* well before the specific blessings of that event are revealed (as they inevitably are, in his experience). Since he is no longer capable of experiencing suffering as something "bad" or "wrong" (though, of course, it remains unpleasant) and is grateful for literally everything, he is perhaps one of the few people on Earth who can honestly say that everything happens for the best. That statement is true *if and only if* it expresses someone's direct experience; otherwise, it is an absurdity. In that person's experience, this is the best possible world because for them, what *is* is always better than a thought about what could be.

While I don't claim a perfect or constant realization of this truth, I too experience deep trust in the pattern, a trust that is rarely shaken by painful or challenging events. I look forward to the day when it is *never* shaken, and I know in my bones such a state is possible. The trust in life that I experience, while not yet 100 percent, is already the most precious fruit of my entire spiritual practice. The most fulfilling kind of trust in life is surely the felt-sense that any painful event is pregnant with blessings, giving rise to gratitude even before those blessings are revealed.

Spirituality or Religion?

In this discussion, I allude to states of consciousness in which one directly (that is to say, nonconceptually) senses the truth of things. How is this different, then, from the kind of person who ignores the facts and clings to "what feels true for me"? It *is* different, I argue, in a subtle but deeply important way. In the latter case, one is emotionally attached to the feeling that arises when a certain proposition is believed. A person might feel so right about believing a certain proposition that they cling to that belief despite lack of evidence or contrary evidence. This is very different from what happens when we successfully *strip away beliefs* and find ourselves thrust into the raw naked is-ness of life, which consists entirely of that which is true whether we like it or not and that which is true whether we believe it or not. This mode of consciousness is nonconceptual (*nirvikalpa* in Sanskrit) in the sense that it is a mode of direct perception free of assumptions, judgments, and unwarranted interpretations. This mode still retains what neuroscientists call predictive coding, so it's not utterly nonconceptual, of course, but it is subjectively suffused with wordless clarity, sparkling awareness, and a kind of piercing insight that can be formed into a variety of verbal expressions but cannot be captured by them.

When Billie Holiday sings about the old folks who say "everything happens for the best," she's talking about a comforting belief that God has a plan and it's a good one, a belief the old folks are advocating for. She very much wants to believe them, because this proposition *is* comforting for anyone who can manage to believe it. But let me restate the difference between religion and spirituality: the former consists of *comforting beliefs* and the latter consists of the *willingness to strip away beliefs* to see what's really true.

How unbelievably fortunate we are to live in a world in which it's really true that every event in our lives contains the potential to confer gifts and blessings in proportion only to the intensity of the event. The question now is, are you going to be satisfied with just believing that, or do you want to directly experience the level of reality where it's as undeniably true as the greenness of the grass or the wetness of rain?

CONTEMPLATIVE EXERCISE

Finding the Blessing

This practice takes patience. It's fine just to do the first part for a few days (or weeks), before you move on to the second and third parts.

1. **The still point.** Get settled and take a few deep breaths. Intuitively find your somatic center: it's about midway between the pelvic floor and the crown of the head, and midway between the front and back of the body (or perhaps slightly more to the back). Many people experience it just below or behind the emotional center in the middle of the chest. Once you've found it, let your attention come to rest there. You might notice that this point is absolutely still: experience swirls around it, but it never moves. It's the point of absolute repose, where consciousness comes to rest within itself. Just breathe, and rest in the center.

2. **Digesting emotions.** Once you're centered, you can turn your attention to your undigested emotions. You might need to recall a situation that's been challenging for you lately to access those emotions. Then practice feeling whatever you feel while laying aside the story about it. That is to say, let go of labels and rationales and feel the raw emotion fully. Once it's fully felt, bring it into the center and let it dissolve into your pure beingness. If another wave of emotion arises, go through the same process again. After it's complete, you'll notice you feel a sense of having been cleansed and/or a feeling of relief and/or freedom.

3. **Open to the blessing.** Begin this stage with a sense of pure unknowing, free of assumptions, and in that sense ask your inner wisdom "What is the blessing of this challenging situation?" Don't try to find an answer with the mind. Just let it come naturally. Perhaps it doesn't come in words at first. Try not to grab on to it. Let it slowly be revealed.

NEAR ENEMY #9

Find Your Soul's Purpose

IN THE ALTERNATIVE SPIRITUALITY SCENE, the idea of "finding your soul's purpose" or "giving your unique gift" or "discovering what you're meant to do" is popular. Indeed, it is treated in many communities as a truism that is almost totally unquestioned. Let's explore the problems with this idea and then consider the spiritual truth to which it is a near enemy.

The idea of the soul having a purpose implies that there is something you need to accomplish in this life to render it truly meaningful and worthwhile. But if this is the case, it is necessarily also the case that you could fail to find and fulfill your soul's purpose, in which case you will have failed at life. Though this odious implication is not part of the popular discourse on the subject, it is palpably present in the anxiety I sense in many people (especially those approaching midlife) and in the corresponding pressure they put on themselves to ascertain their soul's purpose or discover what they are "supposed to do" in this life. Furthermore, many of these people have the strange idea that finding their soul's purpose will necessarily lead to abundance and prosperity, financial and otherwise, almost as if they expect the universe to reward them for finding their soul's purpose. These ideas sow the seeds of much future suffering if it is *not* in fact the case that your soul has a purpose, that you are supposed to learn specific lessons, or that success can be guaranteed by discovering some hidden fact about the nature of reality (e.g., your soul's supposed purpose).*

Your Soul Is Already Perfect

Nondual spirituality teaches that your soul—better to call it essence-nature, true nature, fundamental being, or natural presence to avoid conflation with Western religious ideas about the soul—is always already perfect, being eternally one with Divine Consciousness, the universal power of awareness that expresses as each apparently individual embodied consciousness.** Your "soul" or essence-nature by definition needs no purpose: it is always already complete and whole in itself, full and fulfilled, an exquisite

*The idea that you were born in the place and time you were and to the parents that you were to learn specific lessons effectively devalues human life by implying that your purpose is to "learn lessons" and that your worth is based on successfully doing so. Such nonsense undermines our ability to discover the inherent value in life that is present in each and every moment.

**On this view, consciousness or awareness is said to be *divine* in reference to what meditators discover about the real nature of consciousness: that is unbounded, noncontingent, autonomous, prior to, and transcendent of categories like time, space, and form, and also transindividual and monistic (i.e., there is really only one consciousness by virtue of participating in which all sentient beings are conscious to whatever degree that they are). For this reason, using pronouns like *it* to refer to essence-nature is problematic, because such a pronoun falsely implies that the soul is a distinct and independent entity of its own, when in fact, on this view, something close to the opposite is true—essence-nature, being one with divine consciousness, is undivided from the whole of reality.

vibration of the One that derives its fulfillment from simply *being*. This, at least, is what meditators discover.

On this view, then, the purpose of life is successfully fulfilled in the living of it. Your intrinsic worth is proven by your very existence and could not be proven by anything else. The pattern of existence includes you because it had to, and by simply existing as you do, you fulfill your part in the pattern.

To fully and completely simply *be* is the ultimate expression of your human nature. You cannot fail at life, but you *can* fail to recognize your true nature and thereby fail to fully inhabit your natural state of *being*. If that's what happens, it's perfectly okay since you are what you are whether you realize it or not, but it would also constitute a missed opportunity (from your point of view, anyway) since you probably crave the deep fulfillment such realization brings. In fact, you've probably been looking for that deep and lasting fulfillment everywhere except where it can be found: as an intrinsic property of your essence-nature.

The idea of "soul's purpose" is, I would argue, a piece of Christian theology in disguise, namely the concept that "God has a plan for you." This idea has no place in a nondual view, in which God is not a person or a consciousness separate from your own (see "Nonduality," page 229). But more importantly, the idea that you can and should discover your "soul's purpose" reinforces a sense of lack, fosters anxiety, and disallows the realization of the perfection of your being that is *now*.

That said, there is a truth in relation to which the idea of "finding your soul's purpose" is a near enemy. We all have a longing deep within to realize the truth of our being (which is the truth of *all* being), whether that longing is consciously felt or not. Existential angst is nothing but the unconscious expression of that very longing. Considering this teaching, we might say that our "soul's purpose" is to awaken and realize the truth of our being. This of course is a "purpose" or opportunity common to us all.

Many people want to know what form of expression in the world is in greatest alignment with their essence-nature, presuming that the latter is somehow distinct or unique. But the great spiritual traditions teach us essence-nature is one and the same for all beings (and this truth can be verified in your direct experience, if you go far enough on the path of meditation). And yet here is a seeming paradox: even when all the impediments created by cultural conditioning are removed, the universal essence-nature of all beings does express uniquely through each body-mind. But you cannot be sure that you know what life wants to do through you until you are fully awake to essence-nature. And even then, the knowing is not of a conceptual kind—you discover what life wants to do through you by allowing the spontaneous flow of life-energy to express itself.

So even though we all realize the same unitary essence-nature, the same universal free and independent consciousness, that consciousness expresses differently through each one of us. Embodied realization (*jīvanmukti* in Sanskrit) removes the barriers to that expression, bringing about a natural alignment of action in the world with essence-nature. When such alignment is firmly in place, it will appear to others that that individual has "found their soul's purpose." But the soul has and needs no purpose apart from the natural and spontaneous unfolding of life in each moment. When the impediments to the spontaneous dance of essence-nature are removed, its dance comes into full expression, and every moment of that dance is completeness, is fulfillment.

A dance is not rendered meaningful only by its final movements, and a human life is not rendered meaningful only by accomplishment.

A dance is not rendered meaningful only by its final movements, and a human life is not rendered meaningful only by accomplishment. Accomplishment, when it occurs (and it is only ever "accomplishment" in the eye of the beholder), is simply one possible side effect of a life well and fully lived. And, in the nondual view, any life in which one knows *the nature of being* and allows it to dance in the ways that it does is a life well and fully lived, even if that life entails no achievement, accomplishment, or recognition according to the cultural values of the era.

Therefore, I entreat you, forget about finding your soul's purpose and become dedicated to finding your soul—which is only a figure of speech for your true nature, which in truth need not be found because it never was lost. It's already right here, right now, waiting to be recognized, like a stereogram image you have yet to see. It's pure being-awareness-presence: the power by which you're aware of anything at all.

CONTEMPLATIVE EXERCISE

Sensing Natural Presence

Get settled, relax, and take a few deep breaths. Notice your thoughts. Notice your feelings. Notice whatever you notice. Then bring attention to what is noticing. That which is aware of what is. Don't you find that your very being is made of awareness? It can hardly be made of anything else since everything else comes and goes, right? Check this in your direct experience. When the beingness that you are notices itself as awareness, we could call that natural presence. When you experience natural presence, there's no subject versus object. There's just being-awareness-presence, regardless of what phenomena are arising in the field of perception. See if you can simply enjoy being in awareness-presence for a while. It's what you always are, always have been, and always will be.

NEAR ENEMY #10

You Create Your Own Reality

THIS PARTICULAR MISUNDERSTANDING of nondual spiritual teachings has been around for decades, especially in the New Age scene, which popularized it.* This verbal meme comes in a variety of flavors. At worst, it is the most immature kind of magical thinking (the belief that one's thoughts by themselves can bring about effects in the world) combined with narcissistic entitlement. At best, it is a proper near enemy of the truth, one that can sometimes serve as a temporary ally.

Nondual spiritual traditions tell us that there is a seamless unity between matter and spirit, and likewise between yourself and the Divine. That which appears to be two is in fact one. This is the meaning of the word *nondual* (see "Nonduality," page 229).

*In fact, the roots of the ideas covered in this chapter are much earlier than many suppose: the New Thought movement, which later became called New Age religion (though its adherents deny that it is a religion, scholars disagree) began in the nineteenth century, and the law of attraction was first taught in W. W. Atkinson's book *Thought Vibration: The Law of Attraction in the Thought World* way back in 1906.

The ancient Indian scriptures called the Upanishads teach about the underlying ground of being, the subtle essence-nature of reality that cannot be described in words yet constitutes the "self" of this whole world, and then they declare that is what you are (*tat tvam asi*).* And along the same lines, one who has realized his or her true nature may declare "I am the Absolute" (*aham brahmāsmi*) or "I am Shiva" (*śivo'ham*) in these Sanskrit texts. But in these statements, everything turns on the assumed referent of the given pronoun: to what does the word *I* in the previous statements refer? If it refers to personal identity, then we rightly judge the one making such declarations delusional. If it refers to the impersonal, transindividual, and transcendent ground of all identity, belonging to no one and everyone, then the very same declaration may express authentic truth-realization or enlightenment.

The problem is this: on the simulated version of the spiritual path enabled and validated by the modern spiritual marketplace, people learn to craft a highly developed, refined, and "spiritualized" version of the ego-self, or mentally constructed identity (see "Ego," page 215). They polish it and polish it with endless workshops, retreats, mindfulness courses, and self-improvement books, until it is so refined that it is much easier to deify—that is, much easier to mistake for the transcendent and ineffable transindividual self.

The Spiritual Ego

The spiritual ego is often more harmful than the ordinary ego because it is so much better disguised and therefore more insidious. In other words, since spiritual teachings, like anything else, can be used to inflate the ego, it is entirely possible that a self-deluded

*Referring to the sixth division of the Chāndogya Upaniṣhad in particular.

person does more harm to themselves and others after discovering spirituality than before.

One of the common conceits of the spiritualized ego is that one has a special connection to the Divine, or to Source, and since that is so, one should be able to "manifest" the objects and goals one desires simply through visualization and positive thinking. After all, since God is the creator and we are God, should we not be able to manifest whatever we can dream? Do we not each create our own reality? Well, yes and no.

The pervasive misunderstanding of this teaching has given rise to harmful ideas such as the so-called law of attraction, popularized by the pseudodocumentary *The Secret* (2006), and the broader concept of "manifesting" found throughout the alternative spirituality scene. I argue that these concepts are gross distortions of nondual teachings that are harmful for anyone who holds them because they partake in delusional magical thinking that inevitably brings disappointment and other forms of suffering. They are harmful for society at large because they unwittingly legitimate unearned privilege and the inequities of the status quo (by implying that anyone who thinks positively enough can become prosperous, so those who don't must not be trying hard enough—and other such odious doctrines).

These two forms of harm are inextricably linked. If a person believes they can manifest whatever they like through the power of positive thinking and personal will, that belief will be much less often disconfirmed if they are a person of privilege, whether that privilege takes the form of social status, family money, or simply belonging to the dominant cultural group (e.g., in the Western world, white heterosexual men). Due to this person's unearned privilege (which is largely invisible to them), they will get what they want more often than others, and if they attribute this to the power of their mental states and personal will—as they are trained to do in the law of attraction paradigm—then they will inevitably look at less privileged individuals with a feeling of pity laced with contempt. After all, if other people would only empower themselves with positive thinking and sufficient self-esteem, they, too, could have almost anything they want!

The problems with this view run even deeper than that. Not even the most privileged person can manifest anything they want, but if they embrace the law of attraction teachings, they must always find fault with themselves when the manifestation practice does not succeed: they must not have thought positively enough, they must not have visualized clearly enough, their intention must not have been pure enough, or they didn't believe in themselves enough. Thus, the person ends up with an ego painfully at odds with itself. On the one hand, they think of themselves as gifted, special, powerful, a "manifester;" on the other hand, painful insecurity and angst lurks under the surface. They secretly know that they aren't good enough, because if they were, they would be able to manifest anything their heart desired.

Law of attraction believers are forced by the logic of their own belief to blame themselves for everything unpleasant that happens in their life. They don't often admit this openly, but we see the influence of this doctrine on those who ask themselves things like "Why did I attract this negative person into my life?" The law of attraction doctrine implicitly makes everything that happens to you, good and bad, your fault. But self-referencing every event—that is, crediting and blaming oneself for everything—is simply delusional in an adult. This way of thinking can be normal for a small child, but true adulthood requires us to move beyond compulsive self-referencing and magical thinking.

Law of attraction believers are forced by the logic of their own belief to blame themselves for everything unpleasant that happens in their life.

I hope you see how harmful these ways of thinking are. But clearly, millions of people do not. Witness the veritable landslide of books sold by Esther Hicks, who claims to be periodically possessed by a group of nonphysical beings from another galaxy who call themselves Abraham and who are the putative source of Hicks's teachings. As far as I can tell, every single one of the doctrines propounded by Abraham is a near enemy of the truth at best, and these harmful teachings have been swallowed and perpetuated by countless people to the detriment of our society and spiritual communities. Even if you believe in the New Age doctrine of channeling, there is no compelling reason to believe that the nonhuman beings allegedly being channeled are necessarily enlightened or have our best interests at heart. Perhaps they take delight in toying with credulous humans as a child plays with its dolls!

But let's come back to the main point. It's simply false and even absurd to say you create your own reality if "you" in that sentence refers to the individuated personality-self. What you experience, both in terms of what happens to you and how you react to it, is determined by countless causes and conditions you did not choose (such as your genes and your childhood experiences), which are themselves determined by prior causes and conditions, in a vast web of interdependent interrelationships far too complex for our brains to comprehend. Our experience of reality is created by that vast web of interdependent interrelationships.

The seemingly obvious fact that no one chooses their childhood conditioning constituted such a problem for the Western version of "You create your own reality" that it led to the development of an additional doctrine within New Age thought, the idea that souls choose their parents before birth and choose the lessons that they will learn in that lifetime. This idea has no basis in Eastern traditions.* It provides evidence that New Age thought is truly religious in nature because here we have a nonfalsifiable dogma that continues to circulate despite the fact that a little critical reflection easily yields the realization that if someone already had the wisdom to know

*The primary sources within Buddhism that seem to provide a slight basis for this doctrine discuss how the soul is *karmically compelled* to "choose" its parents.

which lessons they needed to learn in the future, then they wouldn't need to subject themselves to the kinds of painful experiences we go through when we learn things "the hard way." The New Age doctrine pictures souls as effectively enlightened between lifetimes—why would anyone choose unenlightened embodiment?

Now you may say, "I agree that I can't control what happens to me, but at least I can choose how I react to what happens." Believing this sets you up for more self-hatred because, for the most part, you can't choose your reactions—they just happen, and life is probably showing you that every single day. (For more on this, see "You Can Choose How to Respond," page 101).

Perhaps the ultimate fruit of the spiritual life is the actualization of a paradigm of being in which you have access to innate joy and a sense of well-being regardless of your external circumstances. This capacity to be joyful or contented regardless of external circumstances is emphatically not the result of any degree of positive thinking. It is the result of learning how to abide in your essence-nature of pure awareness-presence, conjoined with the patient and dedicated practice of being with what is, a practice that entails becoming crystal clear about the difference between what is and your stories about it.

So, what could possibly be the truth in relation to which "You create your own reality" is a near enemy? I would say that there are two significant truths that are adjacent to this near enemy.

First, when well-interpreted, the teaching "You create your own reality" seeks to empower the practitioner with the realization that their moment-to-moment experience of reality is much more due to internal causes and conditions generated by the body-mind than due to external ones imposed by the environment. Your psyche, your neurology (meaning, how your brain is wired), and even your gut bacteria influence your experience more directly than the events of your day. Or haven't you noticed that the same events affect people differently? This realization is at first sobering, or even overwhelming, because changing one's own biochemistry and psychology can be much more difficult than changing one's outer circumstances.

Understanding the truth that your experience is determined largely from the inside out rather than from the outside in can at first feel like a burden more than a gift—or both simultaneously. But once you realize that your experience of life is not anyone else's fault—and is more determined by your genome, your unresolved past experiences, and your psychological conditioning than anything else—you find that you have the choice to do the inner work that will manifest a less reactive or less negative version of yourself, one who is able to abide much more frequently and steadily in your center, your essence-nature. Ultimately, you're empowered by this realization.

Now, I'm not saying that you *should* do this inner work (since all shoulds are culturally contingent mental constructs), but it's important to know that it is possible to reshape your inner world, which then massively impacts your experience of the external world. In this sense, then, with hard work (in the form of introspection, contemplation, meditation, psychotherapy, and/or somatic therapy, for example), you can in a sense "create your own reality." That is, you can create the conditions that are both necessary and sufficient for a very different (and much more salutary) experience of reality.

But there's a second and even deeper truth adjacent to this near enemy. Here I must issue a caveat: depending on whether you've had a direct experience of what we call the ground of being, and/or of the absolute unity of all phenomena, the words that follow might sound like profound truth or total nonsense.

As noted above, nondual spiritual traditions teach that each of us is an incarnation of the Divine, the infinite, nonpersonal consciousness underlying and pervading the whole of reality. And some nondual traditions, such as Shaiva Tantra, also teach that the divine consciousness from which you are not at all separate or different emanates the whole of reality. In this sense, then, you create the entire reality of all that you experience.

But we must be very careful here: the "you" that creates reality—that is, the sum total of all the phenomena that you experience—has nothing in particular to do with the you *you* think you are—the socially constructed ego-self named so-and-so. In fact, possibly the best word we could use to name your deeper nature, the "you" that freely emits and sustains and dissolves your conscious experience of reality, moment to moment, is *God*. In nondual philosophy, the term *God* refers to the universal, transindividual awareness in which all conscious beings participate and by virtue of which all conscious beings have whatever degree of consciousness they do. It's not the case, in this teaching, that you have two selves, a so-called higher self in addition to the ego-self named so-and-so. Rather, the ego-self that you think you are doesn't even exist as a thing. It is nothing but a mental construct, which is why it is wholly incapable of doing anything but carrying out its programming. It is a program running on the hard drive of your brain. It can't choose anything but whatever it is conditioned to choose—though its programming includes a cognitive illusion by which it conceals its lack of free agency from itself.*

In other words, that which you truly are emanates the whole universe of experience, including all you see and touch as well as everything you think you are (body, thoughts, emotions, etc.), all of which is no more "you" than any other feature of experience (sky, earth, sun, etc.). All that you think you are is merely an appearance within what you actually are (the undefinable vastness of awareness itself), just like everything else. So, you—the real You—does create reality because consciousness is the one and only source of all conscious experience.

The process of spiritual awakening (see "Enlightenment," page 201) entails the progressive melting of the constructed/imagined self into the wider and deeper selfless awareness-presence that

---

*As nondual Tantric philosophy puts it, individual agency *must* be an illusion because there is in fact only one Source of all activity: the transindividual nonpersonal consciousness that is your real nature and that of all beings.

you already fundamentally are. With practice and cultivation, this melting reaches a tipping point beyond which you experience the dissolution of what-you-think-you-are into what-you-are every time you sit for meditation. And then you start to experience it spontaneously, many times a day. And finally, a day comes when the contracted ego-self simply doesn't have enough energy to put itself back together again. This is what we call liberation, the culmination of the awakening journey.

At some point in this process, you experientially realize that what-you-are creates (emits from itself), sustains (holds within itself), and dissolves (reabsorbs into itself) absolutely everything in the whole universe of experience.

In the phrase "You create your own reality," what are the words *your own* doing there? In terms of the true nature of things, they constitute a simple falsehood, for nothing is yours. There is no actual ownership, not even of "your" body or "your" thoughts. It's just a temporary localization of universal phenomena, like a whirlpool in the ocean. Everything you think is yours is all on loan, and it will all be given back. Not even your most heartfelt emotions are yours—they are temporary localized expressions of a universal human experience. Everyone has those same emotions at some point or another—so in what sense are they "yours"? I know they feel personal, but that apparent feeling is actually just a believed thought—an unexamined thought that compulsively self-references the emotions.

Of course, the fact that nothing is personal shouldn't be used as a pretext for spiritual bypassing—pretending that because nothing is yours per se, there is no such thing as responsibility, or no work to be done. If we're honest with ourselves, we find that this inner work, which has the power to transform our experience of everyday life and the way we relate to others, is very much called for. Something calls us to it for the benefit of all beings. The pattern of reality inclines—even pulls—toward harmony, so much so that you must expend energy if you want to resist that pull. To resist it, you must numb yourself with dependencies and distract yourself with countless agendas, large and small. You know what that's like: getting on with business of life, ticking off boxes on the to-do list that never seems to get shorter, doing all sorts of things that you've convinced yourself are important but will mean nothing to you when death comes to call, while occasionally, in the apparently meaningless private moments sandwiched between flurries of activity, catching glimpses of the possibility of something much more meaningful, something sublime that would cast a new light on everything . . . and then it's gone, the glimpse snowed under by hustle and bustle of the estranged and deranged lives that we've somehow been convinced are normal—and so it goes, until that beautiful, heart-opening, life-changing moment that consciousness is ready to wake up to itself through you, as you, for you, and for the benefit of all beings.

NEAR ENEMY #11

You Can Choose How to Respond

IN SPIRITUAL COMMUNITIES these days, one frequently hears "You can't choose what happens to you, but you can choose how to respond to it." A more subtle and sophisticated version of the same idea is "You can't choose how you react, but you can choose how to respond." That is, you can't choose your initial internal reaction to an event, but you can choose your subsequent response, including your speech and action. Let's examine how this is a near enemy of the truth.

According to nondual Tantric philosophy, linear time is an illusion: everything moves in cyclical patterns, and all those patterns interlock and interact with each other in a rhythmic symphony of incredible complexity and incredible regularity. Any given event is always a part of this already-existing pattern. If we ask what caused any given event, the only true answer is "everything" because that's how complexly interwoven the pattern of reality is. The cause of anything is everything. Every feature of reality is so thoroughly interdependent with every other feature, we can say that everything had to be just as it was for any given thing to be as it is. Everything affects everything else, so when we look at the unfolding of events as they appear to us from our limited perspective that sees time as unidirectional and linear, there seems to be a cause-and-effect sequence. It's much more accurate to say that everything is spontaneously unfolding in relationship with everything else—we could even say in dependence on everything else.*

Now, people who embrace the philosophy of individualism (nearly everyone, these days) like to imagine that they somehow stand apart from all this as a free agent. Even though everything else is deeply embedded in determinative causes and conditions, you would like to imagine yourself as a ghost in the machine who has something called free will.

This is, of course, sheerest nonsense.

But precisely how it's nonsense is not easy for most people to understand. When they hear me or anyone else** say that free will is an illusion, a mere thought construct unmoored from reality, they wrongly imagine that we are suggesting that they are a mere automaton, a kind of puppet whose strings are pulled by deterministic forces beyond their control—and they have no choice in the matter. But that is not the argument being made. You have choice, obviously;

---

*Each event in apparently linear time is dependent on not only all past events but also all future ones. To understand how this is possible, consider the example given by physicist Brian Greene when explaining the "spacetime loaf" in his book *The Fabric of the Cosmos* (chapter 5). An alien being positioned very, very far away from us, would, if he was traveling at a sufficient velocity away from us, be synchronous with events that are in the past from our perspective. But if he reversed direction and started traveling toward us, he would suddenly be synchronous with events that are in the future from our perspective. This is possible because space-time is a single existent reality, and so just as the entire universe is already present (though expanding), likewise, all time already exists, and thus from an absolute perspective what we call the future *has already happened.* (Readers who are physicists will please excuse my simplified explanation that seeks to make the relevant point as concisely as possible.)

**For example, Sam Harris, whose writing and speaking on the subject of free will (both in his published book of that name and in his podcast *Making Sense*) corroborated my own thoughts on the matter and brought further precision to them. I echo some of his insights here.

you choose things all the time. It's just that you can't choose what to choose. Meaning to say, you can't help but find the thoughts and desires that compel you compelling, and you can't help but find the thoughts and desires that disinterest you uninteresting. So, whatever you choose, even though you freely choose it, is always a foregone conclusion, given all the factors at play (such as your genetic code, all your past experiences, and the state of your brain and body at the moment of making the choice).

Let's explore this in more depth, but let's first acknowledge why getting this right matters. If we define *free will* as the belief that "I chose A, but I could have chosen B" (and likewise "He chose B, but he could have chosen A"), then believing in free will (that is, believing that counterfactuals are real instead of merely hypothetical) is very likely to make us less compassionate toward ourselves and others, less patient, less kind, and more enmeshed in a contentious argument with reality. (Because "He chose B, but he could have and should have chosen A.") Believing in this version of free will makes us harshly judgmental and all too willing to condemn ourselves and others (for example, criminals deserve punishment because they could have chosen differently—and we somehow believe this despite how constrained we feel when we make choices we will later call unwise).

When reflecting on the past, this belief can generate both self-hatred and the desire for vengeance. It makes us suffer. (According to Tantric philosophy, believing any existential untruth makes us suffer, and this suffering is optional in the sense that it need not continue past the point when you realize it is optional.) I hope that by reading on, you will see why these statements point toward truth.

Consider Your Conditioning

As socialized humans, nearly all our actions in life are based on thoughts, desires, and fears. And none of us choose our thoughts, desires, or fears in advance. A little self-examination shows this to be true. Most people (and all self-aware people, I would argue) agree that they can't choose what to desire (or fear), but many of them think they can choose what to think. But you can't decide what to think before you think it. No one can. Thoughts simply arise spontaneously as an expression of our conditioning.* If you could choose what to think before thinking it, you would already be thinking it. Likewise, you didn't choose to hold the opinions that you do because you can't help but find some propositions convincing and others unconvincing, and you can't help but find some values worth holding and others not. All this is a product of your conditioning, which I broadly define as the complex interaction of your genetic code with the impressions of your various life experiences.

Especially important in this regard are the narratives and framing habits of your particular social group, which your upbringing, in combination with your genetic code, predisposes you to accept and internalize to a greater or lesser degree, or deny and reject to a greater or lesser degree.** Since your brain formed just as it did, your conditioning crystallized just as it did, and you've had the kind of week/month/year you've had, with all these factors in play, upon what basis could you possibly choose to think other than as you do right now? It should be obvious, upon reflection, that there is no such basis, and there couldn't be. And these thoughts and opinions that you didn't choose shape and determine nearly every single one of your actions. So, in what sense can your actions be considered a product of "free will"? Where, exactly, is this ghost in the machine to be found?

---

*Meaning to say, all discursive thought is expressive of some aspect of our sociocultural conditioning, and it can either be triggered by external cues (social or otherwise, as when something brings to mind an associated thought) or it can arise seemingly out of the blue. But even when arising spontaneously, it is no less expressive of sociocultural conditioning. Here I bracket the possibility that nondiscursive (i.e., nonverbal) thought might not always be expressive of sociocultural conditioning.

**For the role of genetics in this, see Robert Plomin's *Blueprint: How DNA Makes Us Who We Are.*

To summarize, every thought you have arises based on causes and conditions already in place, most of which you didn't choose, and those causes and conditions arose based on prior causes and conditions, none of which you chose. So, everything that happens, every thought and action, arises on the basis of a vast network of causes and conditions over which you have little to no control. This is the meaning of the Buddhist doctrine of *pratītya-samutpāda,* which means that everything arises in interdependence on everything else, and nothing exists separate from that vast network of total interdependence. Nothing ever could.

Consider this: Can you choose whether to believe that 5 + 5 = 10? No. Given that you understand what those four symbols mean, you cannot choose other than to believe the facticity of the equation. If you look at it closely, everything's like that. Including everything that's much harder to quantify. For example, you could not choose the degree to which the painful events in your life traumatized you. And you couldn't choose the degree to which you have healed that trauma as of now, nor could you choose how rapidly you healed. You want to give yourself credit for the healing and assign blame to those whose actions were painful for you, but none of it could have unfolded differently than how it did.

Consider this: Can you choose whether to believe that 5 + 5 = 10?

You also can't choose how you interpret events after the fact. Your interpretation forms automatically based on all the narrative fragments about human dynamics that you have internalized up to that point. If you engage in introspection, another interpretation may arise and you may find it more compelling—and if you do, you will replace your prior interpretation with it, and you'll be helpless to do otherwise. The more compelling interpretation will overwrite the less compelling one automatically.

Now, if you're lucky and you found a healthy version of spirituality and/or psychotherapy, it has given you the tools to construct a new narrative about the painful events of your life, one that allows for deeper and/or more rapid resolution of that pain. But could you choose the degree to which you were open to spirituality or psychotherapy once you found it? Of course not. Your degree of openness was determined by the same kinds of causes and conditions as everything else. The same goes for the rapidity with which you were able to internalize the elements of your new worldview and the depth with which you were able to do so.

Is Free Will an Illusion?

Here the problem lies in how we define *free will.* Setting that term aside for a moment, let me clarify that what I'm claiming is an illusion here is your subjective sense of being an independent chooser—that is, your belief (and concomitant felt-sense) that "I chose A, but I could have chosen B." This is a cognitive illusion generated by the false sense of individual agency, the sense you have that you are the thinker of your thoughts, the feeler of your feelings, and the doer of your actions, and therefore you can think and do whatever you like. But as it turns out, picturing yourself as the thinker of the thoughts is just another thought.* There is no thinker separate from thinking, and likewise there is no doer separate from doing. (You can verify this for yourself through introspection, if you look carefully enough.) And if that's the case, you couldn't have chosen otherwise than as you did (in that moment), because all doing occurs as a result of the relevant causes and conditions.

You tell yourself the story that you're a free agent who could have chosen B (or C or D) instead of A, but there is simply no evidence whatsoever to support this belief, and ample evidence that

*As far as I'm aware, the first Westerner to state this insight is these terms was Alan Watts.

disconfirms it. It's just a thought you want to believe.* You chose A because of all the causes and conditions leading up to that point, and you couldn't have done otherwise. That is, you can't possibly choose anything but what seems like the best option available to you at that time, and that *seeming* is determined by all the various causes and conditions in the background (psychological, physical, and otherwise).

And if you honestly believe otherwise, are you not helplessly believing that? If you rebel against what I've said so far, is that really a choice? Or does it just happen?

Clearly, then, we cannot choose how we internally react to anything. It just happens, and it happens immediately. Is it true that we can, however, choose our subsequent response? Well, yes and no. The availability of a subsequent response different from your initial reaction has everything to do with the time you've spent reconditioning yourself with new and more healthful ways of thinking derived from your therapist(s), teacher(s), and admired peers. (And your ability to choose to recondition yourself in this way is, once again, entirely determined by unchosen causes and conditions.) The more you've reconditioned yourself, the more that alternative response is available to you. But in any given moment, you can't choose the degree to which the healthier alternative is available. Perhaps you see it, but you can't bring yourself to choose it. Or perhaps you choose it easily. Or perhaps it feels as though you were almost able to choose the healthier alternative, but you didn't quite manage it. Whichever of these occurs, nothing else could have occurred in that moment. You couldn't have accessed more clarity, or more willpower, than you did in that moment—or you would have.

Now some people, having seen the truth of what is written above,

---

*Olivia Goldhill, "Neuroscientists Can Read Brain Activity to Predict Decisions 11 Seconds before People Act," QZ, March 9, 2019, qz.com/1569158/neuroscientists-read-unconscious-brain-activity-to-predict-decisions.

have a strange reaction: their mind produces a thought like "So there's no point in doing anything!" But this thought only demonstrates that the process of understanding this is not yet complete.

The fact that you cannot choose anything but what looks like the best option available to you at the time hardly means that choosing is irrelevant. Choosing is the most important thing you do in your life. The fact that a hypothetical AI supercomputer that was fed all the data of your genome and your life experiences could accurately predict what you will choose, every time, in no way implies that you can circumvent the internal process of making a choice.

If you truly see through the illusion of free will, there's no reason for it to trigger fatalism. Rather, this cognitive breakthrough can liberate you from worry, self-judgment, self-hatred, and anxiety about making the "right" choice. Indeed, that is the test by which you determine whether you have truly seen through the illusion of free will: you stop judging yourself and others for your/their choices. You might grieve certain choices that others make, but you are free, truly free, from the belief that you or they could have chosen to do anything differently in the past. You stop believing, forever, that you made the "wrong choice" at any point in the past. And you stop believing that you could make the wrong choice in the future. You understand that you can only make what looks like the best choice from the options that appear to you. And it will always be that way, for everyone. It cannot be otherwise. And that's okay. What we call mistakes or wrong choices should simply be called learning.

"But wait," you might now be saying. "I thought 'You can choose how you respond' was a near enemy of the truth—so what is the truth to which it is a near enemy? Everything I've read here seems to add up to total determinism!"

Well, here's where it gets interesting. The universe isn't totally deterministic. If I understand it correctly, the uncertainty principle in quantum mechanics means that while *almost* everything that happens is (or would be) perfectly predictable if you had all the data on all the antecedent phenomena, not *everything* is (perfectly predictable, that is). And sometimes this tiny effect of uncertainty or seemingly random quantum fluctuations can have large-scale results (for example, it is the reason that all black holes ever-so-slowly evaporate—look up "Hawking radiation" to understand why).

Here's where I depart from scientific consensus and advance my own hypothesis: I believe there is a correlate to this principle of quantum uncertainty on the level of conscious experience. If quantum uncertainty corresponds to a little bit of wiggle room within the determinism of our highly structured universe, then that wiggle room might be leveraged by humans through the faculty of self-reflective awareness (in Sanskrit, *vimarśa-śakti*: the power consciousness has in contemplating itself, or the power that is unique to awareness being aware of itself).

What we call mistakes or wrong choices should simply be called learning.

If I understand her argument correctly, Annaka Harris makes a similar point in her recent book, *Conscious: A Brief Guide to the Fundamental Mystery of the Mind*. She argues that consciousness is, for the most part, simply a witness to the thoughts, behaviors, and phenomena that unfold in our experience, none of which we have any significant control over. All those thoughts and behaviors arise based on prior causes and conditions, and consciousness doesn't change that fact. So, what does it change? Why should there be consciousness at all? There seems, Harris suggests, to be one significant way that consciousness interacts with the rest of reality, one lever that it can pull. When consciousness contemplates itself, it catalyzes thoughts and behaviors that otherwise do not occur. It is no longer merely a witness to the unfolding of conditioned thoughts and behaviors; it becomes a source for new permutations of the pattern by reflecting itself to itself. And this self-reflection may, if it goes sufficiently deep, catalyze the process of spiritual awakening, which somehow manages to lie outside the ordinary matrix of cause and effect—or so the Indian Tantric masters argued.

Here we must distinguish awareness becoming aware of itself from the mind thinking about itself. The second might lead to interesting scientific breakthroughs, but only the first can catalyze spiritual awakening. Unfortunately, the first is very difficult to explain because language is a tool of the mind, and awareness is nonverbal.

Awareness can become aware of itself when all doing temporarily ceases and one spontaneously relaxes into pure being. When awareness becomes aware of itself, it intuitively senses within itself that which classical Tantra calls *icchā-śakti,* the innate power of will. This innate potency is very deep but very subtle. Some scholars translate this Sanskrit phrase as precognitive urge because this type of will arises prior to any specific thought or mental image of a possible outcome. It's intimately related to innate intuition, or pratibhā (see page 52). While pratibhā is kind of like a compass (more like an alethiometer, really) for sensing part of the pattern, icchā-śakti is the innate urge within conscious creatures to contribute to the pattern. But the only way it can be something more than merely the enactment of one's conditioning is through the capacity called vimarśa-śakti, the power by which awareness becomes aware of itself.

How can we engage that capacity? Through a daily practice of meditation, if by "meditation" we mean not focusing one-pointedly on an object or entering into a trance-like state but rather reposing in your true nature as awareness-presence. Through learning how to do this, we begin to sense more and more this possibility that life-energy can spontaneously move through us, prior to any mental image of a desired outcome, in much the same way that a painter might be seized by the energy of inspiration and rush to the canvas and begin working without needing to visualize completed painting. But this spontaneous movement is not always creative in the usual sense of that word: it might prompt you to go for a walk, call a specific friend, or spend a summer on a farm.

To return to our Sanskrit phrases, then, we can simply say that engaging vimarśa-śakti (the self-reflective power of awareness) directly leads to a free flow of icchā-śakti (the spontaneous expression of life-energy in creative or beneficial ways). If these potencies become a part of your daily existence, they produce a radically different experience of life—a sense of limitless openness and total harmony with reality. If you can let yourself believe that's possible, and let yourself want it, the whole spiritual path follows from that.

So what if you can't choose your reactions in any given moment. Keep leaning persistently into your conviction that this total harmony with life is possible put that conviction into practice by sitting quietly with it every day, and little by little, the paradigm shifts. The black hole evaporates. Slowly.

And you can see it shifting. More and more frequently, when you're emotionally triggered you remember to pause, breathe, and reflect on a wider range of possibilities before you speak or act. More and more frequently, you can choose whether to believe your thoughts. More and more frequently, forgiveness and compassion spontaneously arise. More and more frequently, you relax and open to what is instead of resisting it.

This doesn't happen by magic. It happens because you create the conditions in which these possibilities become more and more available to you. And how do you create those conditions? By simply sitting still a little while every day and reposing in your innate awareness. As you repose in it, relaxing into pure being, you begin to sense its inherent freedom. As you repose in it, you begin to sense its subtle precognitive urge, a movement of energy that gently, naturally inclines toward the full expression of that freedom. Reposing in your true nature as awareness-presence automatically translates to greater openness, and greater openness automatically translates to the ability to see more possibilities than before. It's still the case that you can only choose whatever seems like the best option available to you, but now you're seeing more options. Not just seeing—you're truly sensing more possibilities.

You might think sensing more options could be detrimental

because more options can trigger anxiety and choice paralysis when one is acting from the conditioned body-mind. But reposing in your essence-nature as awareness-presence has another impact: the development of your ability to access pratibhā, the innate power of intuition that clearly senses the most beneficial option of all those available, without the need for mental deliberation. No worry, no hassle, no second-guessing, no doubts, and no struggle. This is possible because innate intuition (pratibhā) is not mind-based; indeed, it has nothing to do with the mind but rather is always already connected to the pattern of all life. It is the energy of that pattern as it expresses in human consciousness.

Imagine for a moment how it might feel to be you but free of the tension and struggle to somehow be different from how you are. Imagine the joy of growth happening spontaneously. Imagine being awake to your seamless unity with the pattern of the whole, and in harmony with it.

It's not a problem that you can't ever be different from how you are in any given moment or that you can't really choose how enlightened your next reaction or response will be—you can keep learning, little by little, to repose in your fundamental nature as awareness-presence and integrate that experience into every area of your life.

It's not an exaggeration to say that from the perspective of the spiritual path, until you know how to contentedly rest in pure being, *nothing else matters.* Until this capacity to repose in and as awareness-presence is available to you, you're just endlessly running around, putting out brush fires in your life, grasping after fleeting moments of happiness, and making no actual progress in any meaningful sense.

I sincerely hope that the causes and conditions of your life are such that you can prioritize learning to repose in awareness-presence. And if not, don't feel bad about it. It couldn't be otherwise, right now. And in the right moment, in a moment just like this one, a profound shift occurs. It might be constrained by what we call the past, but looking at the past does not allow you to predict it.

In each moment, in each now, nothing could be other than as it is. May you realize that and be free.

CONTEMPLATIVE EXERCISE

Reposing in Awareness-Presence

—

If you've done the exercise in "Find Your Soul's Purpose" (page 85), now it's time to deepen it. As before, get settled . . . then notice your natural presence. Notice that you are awareness itself—that which simply perceives what is before the mind reacts to the perception. Let your awareness repose in itself. Though you can't see what you are—since you are seeing itself or rather the awareness-power that makes seeing possible—you can be what you are. Repose in your own being. Repose in your own awareness-presence.

Then notice that awareness is not separate from what it is aware of. For example, it becomes the vibrations we call sound. There's no hearer separate from the hearing. There's just awareness-as-sound, which we can call hearing or sound. Awareness also becomes the vibrations we call sensation, texture, and so on. There's no feeler separate from the feeling, except perhaps in imagination. Awareness also becomes the vibrations we call thoughts. There's no thinker separate from the thinking. As you verify this for yourself, you may find that you can repose in awareness-presence no matter what phenomena arise in your experience. You never have to stop being what you are to perceive anything, since it is only ever what you are (awareness) in another form. So let your awareness embrace the totality of experience while reposing in natural presence.

NEAR ENEMY #12

Negative Energy (and Negative Emotions)

THE WORD *ENERGY* IS used in many ways these days, especially in communities that think of themselves as spiritual. It's often used as a synonym for *vibe,* as in "He has really nice energy" or "I just love the energy of your home!" It's also often used in the same sense that premodern people used the word *magic*: to denote an unknown kind of force or power that can accomplish something in the real world—despite the inability of modern science to detect its existence—such as in the phrase "healing energy." Magical thinking remains rife in our society, often exemplified by people who deny that they believe in magic. And in the magical thinking paradigm, since there is such a thing as positive energy that can have real-world beneficial effects, then there must also be something called negative energy that can have real-world detrimental effects. The premodern analogues of this are found in not only Western magical traditions but also ancient Chinese thought, which teaches that there is such a thing as negative qi.*

Science is a method of looking more deeply into things and trying to discover if the way in which we think about something is demonstrably founded in reality. In this sense, science is entirely compatible with contemplative spirituality. Though there is a huge amount of poorly done science, primarily due to bad incentives from the corporate sector, that doesn't mean that the scientific method itself is invalid. In fact, it's the most powerful tool humanity as a collective has ever developed.** In criticizing the imaginary concept of negative energy, I'm coming from a perspective based in the critical thinking standards of the scientific method, which I recommend applying to any and all claims about the putative causes of real-world experiences (we'll explore this further in "Energy Healing," page 149). But the reader should not infer from this that I think the scientific method can give a complete picture of reality. Far from it! The argument here will become clear as we go on.

Magical thinking remains rife in our society, often exemplified by people who deny that they believe in magic.

Here we have to establish what we mean by the word *energy*. There's only one definition of the word that applies across the board,

---

*Bryan W. Van Norden,, *Introduction to Classical Chinese Philosophy* (Indianapolis: Hackett Publishing 2011), 98. In the Indian tradition, we find no precise analogue to this concept since there is no such thing as negative *prāṇa* (the Sanskrit equivalent to Chinese qi). However, premodern South Asian people (and most modern ones as well) certainly believe(d) in magic, including and especially black magic, which has recently been relabeled "negative energy" by modern South Asian hucksters of fraudulent magical cures.

**We can define the scientific method informally in terms of its fundamental principles. First, it involves careful observation and application of rigorous skepticism about what is observed, given that cognitive assumptions can distort how one interprets the observation. Second, it involves formulating hypotheses (conjectures), based on such observations; thirdly, performing experimental and measurement-based testing of deductions drawn from the hypotheses; and fourthly, refinement (or elimination) of the hypotheses based on the experimental findings. This process often needs to be reiterated many times to arrive at something approaching certainty, which is why the response to bad science is always to do more and better science.

in science as well as spirituality: "the capacity to do work" or "the power to transform." (This is also the meaning of *śakti*, the Sanskrit equivalent of the word *energy*.) It's incredibly important to understand that in scientific usage, energy is not a thing; it's an attribute of (some) things. So, energy never exists by itself—it's a property of an object or a system that allows that object or system to perform actions with observable results. For example, the energy provided by the food you've eaten allows you to do the work of lifting an object or comprehending the sentence you are reading right now. Inanimate things generally have potential energy, such as the potential kinetic energy in a heavy object sitting on a high shelf: if it falls off the shelf, it has the power to crush your foot.* Its potential energy is not something magical or mysterious; it's measurable.

Setting Boundaries

In light of the fact that *energy* means "the power to do work" what would *negative energy* mean? It could only mean some as-yet unknown force that drains your energy through some unknown mechanism, reducing your power to do work—whether physical, emotional, or spiritual work. And some people do believe that such a force exists and that there are people who somehow possess this nefarious power: spending time with these negative people supposedly drains of your life-energy. I contend that this belief is false, and that the reason spending time with some people is draining is because of something you are doing or not doing. For example, you

*Common forms of energy include the kinetic energy of a moving object, the potential energy stored by an object's position in a force field (for example, in the case of a heavy object on a shelf, it has potential kinetic energy only because it is in a gravitational field), the chemical energy released when a fuel burns, the radiant energy carried by light, and the thermal energy due to an object's temperature. Note that all these forms of energy are attributes of things or systems; they don't exist independently.

might not be setting healthy boundaries for yourself with this person, and *that* is draining.

So, there's important teaching here: labeling a person (or even a place) as having "negative energy" is a way of avoiding responsibility for your own inner state. I would argue that shifting this paradigm is crucial for one's spiritual life. For example, instead of blaming the other person for draining you, you could take responsibility for feeling drained when you don't tell them the truth about your experience, such as "I'm sorry, but I really don't have the time or energy to listen to you right now" or "I care about you, but honestly I need space from this relationship"—or whatever the truth actually is. *You* choose how much time and energy to give someone. *You* choose whether to draw a boundary. *You* choose whether to speak your feelings and honor your own needs.* And if your response to me is "But I'm afraid that they will get upset or will judge me if I draw a boundary and speak the truth about my needs," then that is where *your* spiritual work lies. You dishonor yourself if you don't draw a healthy boundary *before* you feel drained, and you dishonor the other person if you don't tell them the truth. And please be crystal clear about this: the other person is never the one draining you. *You* are draining you. The responsibility for taking care of yourself lies with you.

Labeling a person (or even a place) as having "negative energy" is a way of avoiding responsibility for your own inner state.

Of course, it's also possible that certain people trigger your *saṃskāras*, those remnants of undigested past experience that lie semidormant in your psyche—and if you don't have the emotional bandwidth to digest those saṁskāras as they get triggered, that can

*Some readers will think that these statements about choice contradict the earlier chapter about the illusion of free will. If so, that's simply evidence that you haven't yet understood the argument there. It's perfectly true, of course, that in certain moments you may *not* be able to compel yourself to draw a boundary with someone, or you may not be able to muster up the courage to speak your honest feelings—but the point here is that the responsibility still lies with you.

certainly feel draining or enervating. In this case as well, blaming the other constitutes a missed opportunity to do valuable inner work.

Or it may be the case that certain people articulate negative thoughts—defeatist, denigrating, contemptuous, or pessimistic thoughts—and if you yourself are liable to believing those sorts of thoughts, then being around those who reinforce them will feel draining and it's certainly better for your mental health not to be around those people.* But in this case, too, the buck stops with you. Even if the other person's language and behavior is utterly reprehensible, your inner state is still your responsibility. And you empower yourself by acknowledging that responsibility. This principle is universally taught in all branches of the Yoga tradition.

I contend that "negative energy" does not exist, and the usage of the phrase constitutes a kind of spiritual bypassing. Nor is there any such thing as an energy vampire—that phrase usually refers to a needy person who's willing to take as much as you're willing to give and who doesn't deserve to be demonized for that. It's your job to shepherd your resources, not theirs. For example, you could say something like "Hey in the future could you ask me how much time I have to give you? Or how much bandwidth I have to hold space for you? Because I don't like having to interrupt you and set a boundary to take care of myself."

More rarely, the term *energy vampire* is used to refer to a highly charismatic and suavely manipulative person who you find hard to resist. Such people are important to avoid, and it's healthy to avoid them. In many developing nations, though, there are those who believe in *literal* energy vampires that can drain your life-energy, even at a distance, through some form of black magic. All the available

*It is doubly draining to be around such pessimistic people if you depend on positive thoughts for your happiness. But even if you're an advanced practitioner who has become free of dependence on positive thinking, you probably still wouldn't choose to be around such negative-thinking people very often because awakened people naturally seek synergistic relationships, ones where we share love, wisdom, and support, and such relationships are usually impossible with relentless pessimists.

evidence suggests that this sort of thing can only impact you if you believe it can, through the power of the nocebo effect (a negative version of the placebo effect). The impact derives from the alleged victim's own psyche.

What about a place? Can a *place* have negative energy? I would want to say no (because how could it?), but I admit there seems to be a bit of mystery here. Some people seem to be able to sense when something horrific has happened in a certain location, even if all physical signs of the event have been removed. As far as I know, no legitimate study has been done about this phenomenon, but it does seem to me that the vibration (for lack of a better word) of a terrible event dissipates quite rapidly in most cases. Usually, when it seems like a particular place has "negative energy" it's because you feel strangely disturbed when you enter that place. But this is almost always because of the psychological associations the place has. For example, if you've escaped the influence of a depressed parent but haven't adequately digested the saṃskāras of that relationship, then being in their house will tend to trigger those saṃskāras and you'll feel drained or disturbed. As a rule of thumb, it's a good idea to avoid those places that disturb you, for whatever reason, until your energy body is strong enough to digest those experiences—just as it's a good idea to avoid the company of those who consistently depress or disturb you until you are stabilized in your essence-nature.

We've covered only half of the ground we need to cover here. Sadly, some people these days use the phrase "negative energy" to refer to negative *emotions*. You may be surprised to hear me say that there is no such thing as a negative emotion. Emotions cannot be intrinsically negative or positive, even though we usually experience them as pleasant or unpleasant. At least some of that preferential difference is based on your conditioning (especially the influence of your childhood environment). For example, the same physiological sensations can be interpreted as excitement or anxiety. If interpreted as excitement, dopamine gets released and we experience the emotion as pleasant; if interpreted as anxiety, cortisol gets released and we experience the emotion as unpleasant. As psychology and neuroscience professor Lisa Feldman Barrett argues, emotions are nothing but interpreted physiological sensations. They are not negative or positive in themselves, though we usually find some easier to productively channel than others, mostly due to our cultural conditioning around them.

There are three kinds of emotion that you are likely to label as negative: emotions that you find unpleasant, emotions that seem difficult to handle or do anything useful with, and emotions that you find draining or depleting.

Emotions cannot be intrinsically negative or positive, even though we usually experience them as pleasant or unpleasant.

Let's take the last of these first. Are emotions themselves ever depleting? The nondual Tantric tradition says no. Emotions are energy, and energy is always enlivening. However, it can certainly seem as if an emotion is depleting, because believing a thought can be depleting, and believing a thought can (and often does) generate an emotion. In this scenario, we wrongly see the emotion as the problem when, in fact, the true cause of our suffering is believing the thought that's generating that emotion.

Believing certain thoughts or narratives, especially disempowering or self-denigrating or hateful thoughts, constitutes what we sometimes call an energy leak. If you can identify the underlying negative thought and see it for what it is, then you may be able to stop believing it, at least temporarily. Then you find that the emotion generated by that thought evaporates, replaced by a sense of spacious freedom, openness, or tranquility.*

Of course, not all emotions are story generated. It can work the other way around: there might be a naturally arising raw emotion

*This works out well for all concerned because *only* if you believe an associated story (like "It's so-and-so's fault I'm feeling this way") will you feel tempted to try to dump your "negative" emotion on someone else (usually in the form of a blame story).

(such as anger or sadness) that is generating a thought, in which case dispelling the thought (by ceasing to believe it) does not dispel the emotion. These sorts of emotions, even if they are commonly labeled as "negative" are intrinsically part of our aliveness, and feeling them fully is cathartic rather than depleting. These are the emotions that don't go away even if we become fully free of stories—and nor would we want them to.

Digesting Emotions

Let's consider some examples. If you believe a thought like "He's trying to sabotage me," it probably generates anger. Or if you believe a thought like "She doesn't love me," it probably generates sadness. Please note, it's not the thought itself that generates the emotion; it's believing the thought. For that reason, disbelieving the thought or story will rapidly dissipate the emotion. (And it's important to note that disbelieving a thought does not mean believing its opposite!) But perhaps the emotion is not being generated by the story but rather being reinforced by it: then disbelieving it will not dissipate all of the emotion. For example, "I was able to disbelieve in the story 'He doesn't love me,' but I'm still sad he hasn't called in four days." If that is the case, you need to digest the emotion to access its energy and life-enhancing power.

I'll briefly review the process of emotional digestion. First, if possible, discard the belief that the emotion in question is negative, bad, or wrong, or that you're wrong for feeling it. You may still feel uncomfortable with the emotion, and that's okay. You don't need to like feeling sad or frustrated or whatever. Simply affirm to yourself, with all the conviction you can muster, "It's okay to feel sad" (or angry, or afraid, or whatever) and *soften* toward the emotion. Bring it in close. Let it *all* the way in. And let it pass through the very center of your being. As it does, it will intensify at first, then you'll feel a kind of release as the emotion becomes pure energy. This can happen in one wave or many. In this way, you digest the emotion and transform it into aliveness. The emotion becomes intensity, neither good nor bad, and the intensity becomes aliveness. Then that aliveness can express in all kinds of wonderful ways.

People say of intense emotions, "I don't know how to handle this." But your job is not to "handle" it. Your job is to digest it. And you do that by peeling off the associated story (if any) and letting the emotion all the way in and through.

According to Tantric Yoga, at the center of your being is an axis of energy (connecting the heart to the belly and the throat) that emotions need to pass through to be fully digested. We use the metaphor of digestion because in this process, as with the digestion of food, some of the emotion converts to pure energy or aliveness and some of it is released from the body. So digestion in this sense is a process of both integration and release. It's important, on this view, to not only let go of so-called negative emotions (as so many spiritual teachers advise) but also digest them so that they contribute to our aliveness.

Once you're able to digest your emotions, you get direct proof that any emotion, no matter how "negative," can add to your total *aliveness* and enhance the joy of being alive. When comedian Louis C. K. learned how to digest his sadness, he realized "You're lucky to live sad moments. . . . I was grateful to feel sad." That gratitude is a key sign of successful emotional digestion.*

---

*To see his 2014 interview with Conan O'Brien, see www.youtube.com/watch?v=5HbYScltf1c . We can only hope that Louis C. K. applied what he learned about emotional digestion to the challenges that later arose in his life when his sexual misconduct came to light. But a legitimate example of emotional digestion is *still* a legitimate example even if it is a rare occurrence in that person's life. This is analogous to the fact that a true statement is true even if uttered by a person who lies more often than not. By the same token, a false statement is false even if it is spoken by someone who is usually a bastion of truth. Our popular culture has seemingly failed to understand this basic principle since we commonly see a controversial person's statement on any particular issue dismissed on the basis of their dubious moral character, when

Now, if you admit that none of your emotions are negative, then you will have to admit that nobody else's emotions are negative, either. But it sure can feel otherwise when that other person is throwing intense emotions at you! What do you do then?

Now we come to one of the most revelatory aspects of this teaching. For a spiritual practitioner, having someone direct any kind of emotional energy at you is a golden opportunity. Throw open the doors of your heart—both the front *and* the back doors—and let all that energy pour through you and add to your aliveness! (And maybe don't make it too obvious how much you're enjoying it.) If emotions are energy, then by definition they have the power to do something. In my experience (and that of many other practitioners), all emotional energy, even anger and hatred, has the potential to amplify your aliveness.

If you're a practitioner of Tantric Yoga, all emotional energy flowing toward you is a gift. Nothing need be shut out. This teaching is initially surprising for many people, and it often requires an internal paradigm shift. Some imagine that it must be an advanced spiritual practice to remain open to whatever is flowing toward you and transmute it into the energy of aliveness. But it's less difficult than you might imagine.

Don't Buy the Story

What can make this practice hard, or even impossible, is when you buy the story the other person is pushing along with their emotional expression. If the other person's story is full of blame and denigrating statements, and you believe any of those thoughts, then instead of energy flowing through you and amplifying your aliveness, it can get

---

in fact that statement has to be shown to be true or false (or neither) on the basis of its own merits or demerits.

stuck. It can feel like a dagger in your heart. But let's be super clear about this: it feels like that not because the other person is doing it to you but because you're believing their story on some level. You can't be hurt by words or emotions without your active participation.

When the process of spiritual awakening reaches a certain point, we discover that believing a thought or a story is a choice. When that point is reached, the practice just described becomes easily available to you, and the whole character of your life changes. In the meantime, you can learn to do the work of unbelieving your thoughts and stories one at a time.* None of that work is ever wasted because it makes it easier to see other's thoughts as thoughts instead of truths, and because that work advances you toward the tipping point past which you nearly always have a choice of whether to believe a thought—yours or someone else's. A thought that is seen for what it is, and neither believed nor disbelieved, has no power over you.**

You can't be hurt by words or emotions without your active participation.

Then you find that you can receive another's emotional energy, whatever it is, without harm to yourself. They have no power to make you suffer, and that's very freeing. But even beyond that, you can receive their sadness or anger or whatever and let it contribute to your aliveness, and if you feel so moved, you can return some of that energy to the other in the form of love or compassion.

If the other person is judging you, remember that underlying any judgment is emotion, usually anger, grief, or frustration. You can discard their judgment while still empathizing with their feeling.

---

*See, for example: thework.com/instruction-the-work-byron-katie.

**Disbelieving, which is a form of rejection, can only occur in the context of the possibility that a thought *might* be true. Disbelief exists only in relationship to the possibility of belief, and vice versa. But from the spiritual point of view, thoughts are not the sort of thing that can be true. They are only ever tools, not truths. Truth can't be spoken in words. So, thoughts are simply effective or ineffective relative to a particular goal, and "highly effective" is the closest a thought can ever come to being true.

Those who are worried about "taking on the other person's energy" are worried about precisely the wrong thing. If you can learn to not take on the other person's story, whatever emotional energy they're sharing becomes a potential source of aliveness when you receive it and let it pass through you. If it's really nothing to do with you, it will simply pass through, enhancing your experience of aliveness as it does so. If it does have something to do with you, it will spark some emotion of your own that you will need to digest (and benefit from digesting). Either way, taking on the other person's energy is, in most cases, an imaginary nonissue.* Some readers will believe otherwise, and so I invite you to experiment with becoming both story-free and an open conduit for the free flow of emotional energy, and I will wager that the experience of "taking on" other people's energy simply evaporates.

Having said all that, I should note here that, sometimes, even if you don't buy the other person's story or believe their thoughts about you spoken in anger, you still find yourself hurting over the interaction. If you're *truly* not buying their story, then I would say that the pain you feel is simply a natural grief that the other person is themselves hurting so badly that they are unable to be loving or respectful. That grief is natural and normal, but it's still yours to digest. You can't bypass that process by blaming it on the other. Having said that, I do of course recommend that you step back from any relationship that is generating more pain or grief than you can digest.

---

*I say "in most cases" because I've seen evidence that *some* of those who are abused in childhood seem to internalize some of the abuser's "energy" in some mysterious way. This then needs to be exorcised at a certain point, such as through somatic experiencing exercises that facilitate its release. In these contexts, I've seen things I can't explain in terms of the theory advanced in this chapter. But this seemingly more literal sense of "taking on someone's energy" is rare and, as far as I've seen, only happens in severe childhood experiences.

Intimate Relationships

How does the paradigm taught here play out in close or intimate relationships? That's a huge topic that we can touch on only briefly here. In my experience, people mostly need to learn how to truly listen to each other. This entails being face-to-face, putting everything else aside, and forming an honest intention to listen, but even more so, it requires the temporary cessation of compulsive self-referencing (focusing on your thoughts and stories about yourself), the temporary cessation of defending yourself against the other person's perceived judgments, and the temporary cessation of needing to correct their version of what happened. If you're doing any of those things, you're not really listening to what's alive in the other person and you're unlikely to experience real connection or resolution.

While listening, if possible, adopt an attitude of loving curiosity. Let yourself get interested in what's really happening inside the other person. Instead of analyzing the supposed truth-value of their story, try to discern the feelings, needs, and values that are alive in them. You don't need to rush to label the feelings, needs, and values; you're just listening for them. Then something magical and beautiful can happen: your holding space in this way supports the other person's digestion of *their* emotions, and that usually results in a willingness on their part to listen to you and support you in the same way. Et voilà! More love blossoms in the space between when you're patient and mature enough to let all the other person's emotions, as well as your own, move through. Love doesn't blossom despite the "negative" emotions; it blossoms because of accepting them and exploring their roots. "Negative" emotions between people are always an opportunity for greater connection or intimacy. In that sense, they represent a profoundly positive opportunity.

"Negative" emotions between people are always an opportunity for greater connection or intimacy.

So far, we've established that there's no such thing as negative energy or intrinsically negative emotions: not in you and not in others. We've learned that even if someone blames you for their unpleasant emotion and tries to dump it on you, that's a gift, if (and only if) you're strong enough to receive their emotional energy and pass it all the way through. But if you're not able to receive their emotional energy and let it pass through because you believe some aspect of the story they're pushing, then that, too, is a gift, despite being painful. How so? Because, on the spiritual path, you need to be shown what falsehoods you're still believing about yourself before you can dissolve them. And remember, someone's story about you only has the power to hurt you if, on some level, you believe it. In which case you are hurting yourself with that underlying belief. And don't you want to be shown your self-limiting beliefs so you can address them and dissolve them?*

Emotional Capacity

A *sādhaka* (spiritual practitioner) who understands these principles and puts them into practice doesn't need to worry about avoiding so-called negative energy, negative emotions, or negative people. All charged human interactions are a potential gift, offering us empowerment and aliveness. But on the other hand, a sādhaka needn't seek out such interactions, either. Why shouldn't they? Because the emotional body, also called the energy body or subtle body (*sūkshma-śarīra* in Sanskrit), like the physical body, has a maximum capacity. If you exceed it, you won't be able to digest any more emotional energy, leaving both parties hurting and depleted. (Which is why acknowledging your limited bandwidth by drawing boundaries with others is so important!) There are practices in Tantric Yoga to

*With some self-limiting beliefs, we need to address them in a supportive context (for example, in therapy) before we can dissolve them.

strengthen the energy body, but it's super important to be humble enough to know your limits because it can severely impact your mental, emotional, and physical health to exceed them too often.

At this point people usually ask something like, "But what about people who are evil?" Can a human being truly be evil? That depends on your definition of the word. If by the phrase "evil person" you mean "someone who is so damaged or deranged that they can do a lot of harm, whether intentionally or not," then yes, there obviously are evil people. But I don't think we gain anything by using that word. When we demonize others, we feel tempted to destroy them, and in that way, we make ourselves more like them. In other words, we become more like those we hate, so it's important to cultivate a deeper understanding of how human beings work, since understanding always mitigates hatred and increases compassion. However terrible someone is, or however terrible some corporation or institution is, we still need less hatred in this world and more love, so it's incumbent on each of us to consider whether we are contributing more to the total amount of love or hatred through our thoughts, words, and actions. Cultivating love for those doing good and lessening hatred for those doing harm is recommended by the Yoga tradition as a practice that is beneficial for you and the world.*

To cultivate understanding of human nature of the kind that mitigates hatred, it helps to remember this maxim: everyone everywhere is just trying to get their needs met the best way they know how. If the only strategies for need-meeting that they know are manipulative and/or violent, that is tragic and worthy of grieving. But such people deserve your compassion, not your condemnation. Of course, compassion does not equal permissiveness or approval.

In conclusion, the joyous culmination of the spiritual life (on the Tantric path, anyway) is the point at which the energy body (a.k.a.

*Here "doing good" is a shorthand phrase for "contributing to the well-being of conscious creatures," so we need not concern ourselves with the fact that words like *good* and *bad* (and even *harm*) are both relative and culturally contingent.

mental-emotional body) is so strong, there is nothing to fear and no situation, person, or place that must be avoided. You're finally free of all unnecessary inhibition and you no longer cringe away from any aspect of life. It's profoundly liberating to reach that point! In fact, it is liberation itself.

CONTEMPLATIVE EXERCISE

Being with "Negative" Emotions

—

Do this exercise when you're feeling an emotion that you would normally label as negative. Get settled and take a few deep breaths. Feel whatever you feel fully. Then strip away the interpretation of it. Drop the idea that you can know why you're feeling what you're feeling; drop even the label you've been assigning to the feeling. Feel it without the story, without the label. Do you notice that the emotion becomes pure intensity? Free yourself from the need to understand what you're feeling, and simply be with the intensity. Then become the intensity. Do you notice that now it feels like pure aliveness? Let that intense aliveness move through you. Perhaps you take a minute to vocalize, shake, or dance around the room. Then come back to stillness. Notice the quiet aliveness suffusing your being. Perhaps you can regard it now as sacred. Sacred aliveness. Breathe a sigh of relief, if that feels natural.

NEAR ENEMY #13

Energy Healing

THE "HEALING" INDUSTRY is booming, and its profits are soaring. I put the word *healing* in quotes here because I'm not talking about actual healing of mental and physical illness through still-inadequate but well-vetted and well-regulated modalities (such as allopathic medicine, physical therapy, psychotherapy, somatic therapies, etc.). I'm referring to the countless forms of so-called energy healing that constitute a multibillion dollar industry* but so far have no compelling evidence of consistent efficacy and yet claim to solve real (and imagined) problems of both mind and body. Here the term *energy healing* is interchangeable with *energy medicine, shamanic healing, quantum healing,* and similar terms.

All these phrases boil down to a simple claim: some special, gifted individuals can feel and manipulate an energy field unknown

*Acupuncture *alone* constitutes a $50 billion (annually) industry worldwide: "Acupuncture Market Share, Size Global Industry Revenue, Business Growth, Demand and Applications Market Research Report to 2023." *MarketWatch.* Retrieved 19 October 2021. Dietary supplements, the vast majority of which have not shown any measurable effect beyond placebo, constitute a $75 billion (annual) industry that is rapidly growing toward the $100 billion mark.

to science that pervades and affects the human body through an unknown mechanism, or some specially attuned people can channel a unique type of energy unknown to science that can accomplish real-world effects. These amount to claims that magic works, *magic* being a word for a domain untouched (and possibly untouchable) by science. We can repudiate these magical claims because anything that works consistently, even if it's only 10 percent of the time, can be shown to work through carefully designed tests (called randomized controlled trials), even if we don't yet understand how it's working. That is to say, the scientific community is open to and interested in the demonstration of any consistent effect, especially effects that are not understood and are therefore likely to attract research grants. Our scientific system, while imperfect, is set up in such a way that if any form of "energy healing" was consistently effective, we would know that by now, and there would be incentives to figure out why.

Am I dogmatically embracing the scientific method and claiming that it can explain everything? Am I claiming that we can know for sure that energy healing never works? Absolutely not, to both questions. All I'm saying is that energy healing, if it exists, doesn't work consistently or predictably. Therefore, those who make specific claims for the efficacy of any form of energy healing are fooling themselves and others. And if they charge everyone who walks in the door the same rate, that's an implicit claim of consistent efficacy, or an implicit claim that the likelihood of effective treatment is reasonably high, neither of which have been shown to be true in the case of anything labeled as "energy healing" or its synonyms.

None of these facts rule out the possibility of outliers—practitioners who are getting consistent, measurable results with their clients, even through completely mysterious means. It's just that we can confidently say that such practitioners are rare enough that they don't produce statistically significant results when averaged against the mass of noneffective practitioners. They don't raise the signal above the ambient noise floor, as it were.

Why, then, are these energy healers found everywhere, in every major town and city? Is it because the general public is so pathetically gullible, so uneducated, and so desperate? I would say no, that's not the reason. The general public in the United States and the United Kingdom is fed up with the limitations of an outmoded health care system that, for the most part, can only deal with the ailments that are both extreme and well studied, and thus has no time for conditions that are difficult to diagnose or are not obviously debilitating. But we need to dig even deeper to understanding why the various forms of "energy healing" are flourishing.

I contend that many chronic physical conditions are somatoform in nature, which is to say that they are either caused or (more commonly) greatly exacerbated by unresolved and largely unconscious psychological issues, probably in the manner outlined by Dr. John Sarno and his collaborators in the book *The Divided Mind*.* But our understanding of how the psyche affects physical health and chronic pain is still in its infancy, so it's easy for more conservative scientists to level criticisms at that book and others like it, though I'm convinced their fundamental ideas will prove to be correct.

Symptomatic Relief

Now, those with chronic conditions that are largely somatoform in nature are likely to feel symptomatic relief from any form of prolonged contact with a sympathetic and caring person, even without physical touch. That symptomatic relief can be greatly enhanced by the placebo effect, which of course is partially dependent on the patient's perception of the caregiver as competent and qualified.

---

*I use the term *somatoform* in place of the outdated *psychosomatic* because of the widespread severe misunderstanding of the latter term. See the Jonas and Crawford piece cited in note 152 for independent evidence strongly supporting Sarno's hypothesis.

Therefore, someone with virtually any sort of chronic condition can feel significant symptomatic relief from something like Therapeutic Touch, Reiki, or acupuncture if they have a rapport with the practitioner and if they believe that the modality is likely to be effective. The second factor used to be thought primary in the placebo effect, but we now know that the former is at least as important.* That is to say, human connection, and sympathetic human presence, is responsible for much of the real-world benefit of the placebo effect. It's important to understand that the placebo effect, contrary to popular belief, is a real effect with real measurable benefits. If you need convincing of this, consider the little-known fact that placebo surgery (that is to say, convincingly faked surgery) has been shown to be just as effective as real surgery in resolving some physiological conditions, especially those related to pain.**

If the practitioner calling themselves an energy healer knows how to hold space well and exude care, they can provide symptomatic relief in the same way a pill can provide relief for physical pain (though through a different mechanism). This is great, but it shouldn't really cost more than a pain relief pill. Having said that, we should note that there is some evidence to suggest that, on very rare occasions, a practitioner of one of these "energy healing" disciplines can intuitively facilitate actual healing (in which case the discipline itself is sometimes a kind of pretext or smokescreen for something

---

*J. E. Charlesworth et al., "Effects of Placebos without Deception Compared with No Treatment: A Systematic Review and Meta-Analysis," *Journal of Evidence-Based Medicine* 10, no. 2 (May 2017): 97–107.

**Listen to this fascinating podcast: www.npr.org/transcripts/718227789; for peer-reviewed evidence, see J. Bruce Moseley et al., "A Controlled Trial of Arthroscopic Surgery for Osteoarthritis of the Knee" *New England Journal of Medicine* 347, no. 2 (July 2002): 81–88, and Wayne B. Jonas et al., "To What Extent Are Surgery and Invasive Procedures Effective Beyond s Placebo Response? A Systematic Review with Meta-Analysis of Randomised, Sham Controlled Trials," BMJ Open 5, no. 12 (December 2015). The astonishing conclusion of the latter meta-analysis: "The standardised mean difference for surgery versus sham surgery was nonsignificant for pain-related conditions." (Because the "sham" surgery was effective, in these cases, for pain relief.)

that happens spontaneously on the basis of deep human connection and the mysterious power of what we can only call loving presence).

If actual healing happens, the difference from symptomatic relief is substantial and obvious: the ailment or condition is no more. It's, you know, healed. With symptomatic relief, the condition can temporarily feel as though it's gone, only to return full-force a few hours or days later. If that happens and the person you paid calls themselves a healer, then by rights you should get a refund because you're not healed. (If they call themselves a symptom reliever, then that's a different story!) Would you not demand a refund from a medical doctor that failed to perform the needed procedure, leaving you no better off than before? (Of course, sometimes medical doctors do charge people despite accomplishing nothing, and that's not remotely okay either!)

What if we reserved the word *healing* for situations in which healing has demonstrably taken place? Remember, one synonym for *healed* is *cured*.* Now, having said that, it is of course possible that partial healing could take place in one of these "energy healing" sessions. But that, too, should be demonstrable: the condition is permanently improved, like a wound being measurably smaller. If you aren't sure whether healing has happened (after a few days), then it probably hasn't. And you certainly shouldn't be paying big bucks for something that you're not sure worked at all beyond the temporary symptomatic relief.

We don't have the space-time for a long excursus into physics, but I do feel compelled to note that many "energy healers" love to invoke the term *energy field* or even *quantum field*. In many spiritual communities, it's accepted virtually without question that people have an energy field that only psychics and energy healers can detect and influence. This imagined energy field escapes detection by even the most sensitive of scientific instruments that can detect

*The verb derives from the Old English word *hælan*, "to cure; save; make whole, sound, and well."

X-rays emitted billions of light-years away or neutrinos, incredibly subtle subatomic particles with almost no mass and zero electromagnetic charge. But somehow science can't detect the energy field that energy healers claim to affect?* This strange supposition only reveals that most people don't know what an energy field is. By definition, an energy field is always measurable—for example, thermal energy exists as a scalar field in which each point in three-dimensional space can be assigned a value we call temperature. If someone speaks of an energy field, the easiest way to test whether they know what that term actually means is to ask "Is it a scalar field, a vector field, or a tensor field?"—those being the different known types of energy field.

Here I seem to be suggesting that all "energy healing" is bogus. So, how is it a near enemy of the truth, which by definition is something close to a real and profound truth? I contend that most people who are suffering unidentified mental and physical ailments (and even some of those suffering diagnosed ailments) don't need healing per se; they just need to learn to more fully digest their emotions and experiences because unresolved and undigested experiences involve unconsciously suppressed emotions that can lead to somatoform illnesses and chronic pain conditions (to put it simplistically).

First, let's address the majority of people who think there's something wrong with them that needs healing: you feel chronic angst, fatigue, and/or mysterious sources of dull and diffuse pain (emotional and physical), so you do cleanses and you go to self-professed healers and perhaps even pay to have your aura analyzed and nonspecific "blockages" removed from your chakras. If this doesn't work, you might go to the next level and pay a "shamanic healer" to retrieve lost pieces of your soul and/or remove invisible but parasitic

---

*Of course, humans *do* have a measurable electromagnetic field—our bodies radiate thermal energy in the infrared spectrum. This, of course, is not what "energy healers" are talking about.

noncorporeal entities."* (For readers not aware of this world, I am not making this up—just google to find "shamanic healers" in your area. This phrase has become shockingly common.)

Emotional Digestion

So-called energy healing is, of course, nearly always a load of (very profitable) nonsense. I propose to you that in truth, your real issue is the same issue that most humans have: emotional indigestion, which is resolvable through basic emotional hygiene.

A little background is necessary to understand this. In classical Tantra, we learn that the subtle body (also known as the mental-emotional body) digests emotions and experiences in much the same way that the physical body digests food—extracting energy and releasing waste. At least, that's how it's supposed to work. However, since most humans receive zero coaching in how to be with their emotions in childhood,** or indeed at any other time, a portion of many of their emotional experiences (especially the most impactful ones) remains, as it were, undigested in the form of what we call saṃskāras (i.e., "impressions"), which are kind of like chunks of unresolved past experience that hang around in the subtle body. (I should mention here that the term *subtle body* is virtually synonymous with the Western term *psyche*, but it is preferable here because it emphasizes the Tantric teaching that the psyche actually interpenetrates the physical body, and thus we often feel these saṃskāras,

---

*Here, the term *shamanic* relates not to any traditional practices of indigenous people but rather to a recently created imaginal world all its own (with tenuous connections to some traditional shamanic ideas), serving a specific cultural demographic that is overwhelmingly white, privileged, and "alternative." Consider this example chosen almost at random, which uses language that has become ubiquitous in these circles: forbes.com/sites/biancasalonga/2021/08/07/shamanism-demystified-enhance-overall-wellness-through-shamanic-healing.

**See the TED talk by Guy Winch, www.ted.com/talks/guy_winch_why_we_all_need_to_practice_emotional_first_aid.

these pieces of undigested experience, manifest themselves somatically more than conceptually.) There can be saṃskāras of pleasurable experiences as well as painful ones, but even the latter are not intrinsically bad for you; in fact, they constitute a source of potential energy that is released through the process of emotional digestion, as already outlined in "Negative Energy (and Negative Emotions)."

Even though saṃskāras are not intrinsically bad, when we accumulate a lot of these undigested remnants of past experiences, it has a significant, detrimental impact on our life experience overall. In the traditional Tantric model, one's life-energy is a finite quantity, and each saṃskāra sequesters a small amount of it, so the more undigested experiences one has, the less life-energy is available, resulting in fatigue, depletion, ennui, angst, loss of passion, and/or a sense of meaninglessness or pointlessness to life. Furthermore, in a person who possesses a critical mass of undigested painful experience, these saṃskāras can, as it were, start to toxify in later life, resulting in bitterness, dourness, rigidity in mind and body, the inability to feel compassion or empathy, and/or other symptoms.*

To be clear, here I'm talking about the "normal" human experience in our society; I'm not addressing the situation of exceptionally traumatized people. But as a society we need to start acknowledging that the "normal" human experience in the twenty-first century is one of considerable chronic suffering, concealed as thoroughly as possible for the sake of social status and image crafting. We are far from okay, but there's nothing intrinsically wrong with us; we just

---

*To the reader who thinks the language used in the last couple of paragraphs is not really all that dissimilar to that which I previous criticized, I would say that what I'm presenting here is a conceptual model validated by its effectiveness; I'm not invested in the question of whether it's literally true. From my perspective, virtually nothing said in words is *literally* true. These are terms of art that are effective in a given context. I'm interested in efficacy. And I'm suggesting here (and at many points throughout this book) that it would be most beneficial if you, dear reader, were likewise concerned with efficacy. Truth cannot be legitimately correlated with what is *pleasing* but rather with what is demonstrably *effective*.

need to learn to digest our experiences. This is harder in the twenty-first century than in previous eras because we don't have (or don't allow ourselves) sufficient time and space in quiet solitude (or with a trusted friend), when for many people, emotional digestion can happen almost automatically. So, we have a backlog of undigested suffering, which spurts out in the almost unbelievable vitriol we see online or gets suppressed and turns into mysterious physical ailments of all kinds. Many of us blame the latter on diet, but I contend that if we can digest our emotions, we'll digest our food better as well, in which case we need not engage in the obsessive forms of selective food avoidance that are increasingly prevalent today.

If we had a sane society, emotional digestion would be an ordinary part of life. No one would think it odd or unwarranted if someone excused themselves in a middle of a conversation or a meeting to go cry or scream for ten minutes (or simply be quiet with their feelings) because everyone would understand that virtually anything in everyday life can trigger a saṃskāra of an old experience, the triggering of a saṃskāra is a golden opportunity for digestion, and all successful digestion adds to your aliveness and your joie de vivre. And, by the way, it need not be a saṃskāra getting triggered that occasions the need for digestion—one can also digest emotions related to the present-moment situation in real time, which also enhances aliveness and avoids the depositing of a saṃskāra, which will need to be digested later.*

Unfortunately, we don't yet live in a sane society or an emotionally healthy world. Most people don't know how to digest their challenging emotions and experiences, so they tend to dump them on others—through blaming, shaming, emotional off-loading, etc.—or they suppress them, shoving them down inside, where they slowly toxify. Additionally, if you believe others are to blame for what you

*For more on this, please see chapter 11 of my book *The Recognition Sutras.*

feel, that inhibits digestion and makes it more likely that you try to enlist those others to do your emotional labor for you.

Emotional digestion happens fairly easily and naturally in the following context:

- You can acknowledge and take responsibility for your feelings (without blaming anyone)—"This is what I'm feeling, and it's totally normal that I'm feeling this, given the situation and my past history; no one's to blame, but it's my job to digest my emotions, since no one else can do it for me."
- You value yourself enough to take some time every day to fully *be with* whatever you feel, giving yourself the space to both feel and digest it.
- You can recognize that your stories about what you feel are just that—mental fabrications that seek to explain the feeling and thus gain an illusory sense of power or control over it, and you recognize that believing these stories inhibits emotional digestion.
- You can lay the stories and interpretations aside and bring the raw feelings in close, welcoming them into your heart, while affirming your ability to digest them—"I welcome this feeling, whether or not I like it. I permit it to pass over me and through me. I let myself feel it fully. I'm not trying to get rid of it too soon, and I'm not hanging on to it. I can digest this. And when I do, I become stronger." (I'm not suggesting you repeat exactly these words; I'm trying to point toward the kind of attitude that is effective.)

Emotional digestion needs to happen almost every day. Healing work, on the other hand, is what is called for when someone has a physical or emotional wound sufficiently deep that it needs special attention. Without such attention, it becomes life-threatening. Emotional wounds become life-threatening when they sap the joy out of life and begin to paralyze one's life-energy. Perhaps someone with a very strong psyche can heal themselves of deep emotional wounds, but most people need some assistance and support. For example, the inability to forgive yourself for hurting someone, or the inability to forgive someone for hurting you (and we should note that that language is almost never accurate—nearly all painful interpersonal experiences are thoroughly co-created) can effectively inhibit the normal digestion process. In this case, one often needs a therapist who can facilitate the understanding that makes forgiveness possible and thus makes digestion of the experience possible.

Intrinsic Wholeness

The type of professional help you engage matters—the right tool for the right job, as it were. For example, if you are consciously or unconsciously terrified of the intensity of your undigested feelings, then you won't be able to access them at will, in which case a somatic therapist might be needed to work with the physical body in such a way as to help you access the buried emotion and feel it fully so it can move through and resolve itself. For some other people, only psychedelic-assisted therapy can help them access what they need to see and feel and digest within themselves to experience their intrinsic wholeness. And here we must note that a therapist is a trained, certified, and licensed professional. A self-appointed "energy healer" operating in a totally unregulated industry cannot substitute for a therapist.

A self-appointed "energy healer" operating in a totally unregulated industry cannot substitute for a therapist.

I've talked about emotional digestion you can do on your own versus the need for professional assistance. But isn't there something in between? Some middle ground where we need a bit of help but not full-scale professional intervention? I would say yes. But this middle ground does not need to be occupied by monetized "energy healing" or "shamanic healing"—we can, as a society, learn to come together and support each other in this way, outside the capitalist model.

Significant emotional wounds that don't require professional intervention can be healed, partially or totally, with the support of a trusted friend who is intuitive and/or emotionally intelligent. If that person can hold space, witness you compassionately, and reflect your experience back to you (without distortion) when needed, they might be able to co-create real healing with you beyond what you can do on your own. No special technique is needed for this: just the intuitive sense of how to dissolve the artificial boundary between two people and feel through stuff together. But it doesn't make sense to charge money for this, because (a) it only tends to work when there is already a bond of trust and friendship, (b) there's no guarantee of it working, and (c) you can't put a price on it. To be effective, it has to be based in the authentic desire for connection and the authentic desire to contribute to another's well-being for the intrinsic value of doing so.

There are many other ways that spiritual friends (*kalyāna-mitras* in Sanskrit) can support each other in the digestion of difficult emotions and challenging experiences. Such methods can be surprisingly simple, such as having your trusted friend rock your body rhythmically in various ways while you moan or sigh or vocalize whatever needs to come out (your friend would need to be okay with weird sounds coming out of you—this is a normal part of emotional release for many people). Another powerful method is to have a friend with a loving heart and a strong voice sing OṂ or some other mantra(s) into the place in your body where the unresolved emotion is stuck (if you know where that is).

These are the kinds of things friends would do for each other as a matter of course in a sane society, and these are the kinds of things friends can do for each other in any healthy community. Such support shouldn't need to be paid for because it requires no special skill (and because it's not something we could ever institutionalize and regulate). If holding space effectively and facilitating healing in this way seems like a special skill, that's only because we are still so very far from a sane society. Perhaps someday everyone will learn these things in school as a matter of course; perhaps someday we'll realize that our primary and secondary schools need to train kids in emotional intelligence, interpersonal communication, real life problem-solving, critical thinking, and emotional digestion rather than subjects that only a minority of those kids will go on to utilize (like math, science, history, etc.).

Doubtless, those readers who consider themselves energy healers will be upset by what I've written here. Drafts of it were very controversial in the community of which I'm a part. I have found that when people's livelihood and/or self-image is involved, they get strongly triggered by arguments that seem to challenge, either. Having already upset those folks, I might as well go the final mile and say this: you're in an unregulated industry precisely because *there's nothing to regulate.* None of these modalities based in undetectable forms of energy that some claim to feel* has been proven to have *any* effect beyond placebo—in other words, beyond the valuable symptomatic relief that happens when (a) one believes or wants to believe that the treatment will work, and (b) one receives the loving touch and/or benevolent care of another human. Based on personal experience with several of these alternative modalities (when I had recurrent lower back pain), I would say that a significant part of the symptomatic relief is due to the fact that the person receiving the treatment often enters a meditative and/or relaxed state that, with a little practice, they could actualize on their own (e.g., through yoga

*I don't doubt the testimonies of many "energy healers" that they feel *something* and that their clients often claim to feel something, but there are alternative explanations for these feelings than the existence of a scientifically undetectable energy that has real-world effects. So please understand, I'm *not* calling you a liar if you claim to be an energy healer or the like. I'm claiming that you might be misunderstanding what's happening.

and meditation). I think this is the case even with acupuncture, a modality that many believe to be scientifically proven but that in fact hasn't yet proven its efficacy beyond a consistently strong placebo effect (and here I remind the reader that the placebo effect is not merely psychological—it can sometimes be associated with measurable symptomatic relief, such as decreased inflammation).*

Other people will want to point out that many traditional cultures, including Tibetan culture, teach a kind of spiritual healing that might well be called energy healing. But let's be clear about this: these are modalities whereby shaman-type figures attempt to heal actual ailments of the mind or body (like malaria or schizophrenia) through *magical or supernatural means* (as well as, sometimes, through herbs and plants). These folks are, in sense, more honest than New Age "energy healers" because they openly acknowledge that they deal in magic, which is at best unpredictable in its effects. And these shamans are traditionally held to a high standard: they are judged as having been successful only if the malady in question actually goes away (i.e., a cure is effected). I think we should apply the same standards to "energy healers" in the West. In fact, to avoid hypocrisy, we must apply the same critical standard to traditional and modern claims of efficacy.

"But," I hear some of my readers objecting, "don't you teach so-called energy-body practices as part of Tantric Yoga?" Yes indeed. The difference—and it's a huge difference—is that there are no claims of healing power being made. Nor are there implicit promises of enlightenment. I don't teach that the subtle body practices of traditional Tantric Yoga will bring about this or that result. I invite people to try out these practices and discover what the results are for them because I know that results of any given spiritual practice can vary widely from person to person, and what seems to work miraculously

*So, to say that a specific intervention has been shown to have no effect beyond placebo is *not* to say that it has no measurable physical effect! It's to say that the measurable physical effect is likely due to the relaxation response and other psychological factors.

well for one does nothing at all for another. Additionally, I want to avoid, as far as possible, the effects of priming, the phenomenon whereby someone primed to have a particular kind of experience and who wants to have it imagines they do have it but with no actual lasting beneficial impact.

Indeed, the purpose of the practices of Tantric Yoga is not to have an experience at all but rather to bring about a gradual, inexorable, powerful paradigm shift that is nonconceptual yet utterly indisputable (to the one who undergoes it). Of course, in that process of paradigm shift we call awakening (see page 182), moments of spontaneous emotional digestion, and even moments of deep healing, can and do occur as a wondrous side effect of the process.

And yes, it's also possible that those rare individuals who go as far as one can go with the Tantric energy-body practices may develop the capacity to accomplish things through some means that science cannot yet explain, up to and including healing cancer and HIV. Such accomplished masters can also demonstrate other powers that should be impossible according to science, such as delivering messages to people in dreams or visions, messages that can then be subsequently verified. I've seen these anomalies myself. But allowing for the existence of such very rare outliers does not undermine my argument. Put simply, it's irresponsible to recommend "energy healing" to someone with real mental or physical illness if it has less than a 1 in 1000 chance of effecting real healing (as the evidence—or lack thereof—suggests). And recommending it—and/or unproven herbal supplements and homeopathic "remedies"—instead of conventional medicine and well-vetted therapeutic modalities is worse than irresponsible. It's dangerous.*

---

*Here we didn't delve into the deceptiveness of the multibillion dollar "dietary supplement" industry (which includes herbal supplements, essential oils, and other products not proven to have any effect beyond placebo) or the idea of "homeopathy," which simply constitutes fraud in the case of those homeopathic practitioners who assert that it works on some basis other than placebo. These topics were not addressed here because they have already been thoroughly debunked by professional researchers.

NEAR ENEMY #14

I Am My Own Guru

IN THE 1960S AND 1970S, Westerners were remarkably trusting of gurus, especially gurus from the East. One might say that many were naïve and credulous as well. People didn't seem to have much discernment or understanding of how a very charismatic figure might also be a very dangerous one. But this credulousness also had beneficial effects in some cases. If you are very open and trust a teacher implicitly and that person has your best interests at heart, it can be highly beneficial for your spiritual life because you receive what they have to offer on a very deep level. This was the case in my own life. I was very fortunate that the guru I followed when I was younger, and trusted implicitly, and yes, pedestalized, was interested in nothing but supporting my spiritual unfolding. However, if the guru figure doesn't have your best interests at heart or, even worse, is deluded and possessed by a god complex, then you are in a dangerous situation indeed.

The number of fraudulent and half-baked gurus proliferated in the 1970s, and things took a very dark turn with Jim Jones's Peoples' Temple cult, culminating in the infamous 1978 mass murder-suicide at Jonestown. This event was the most effective possible demonstration of the worst-case scenario in abdicating one's sovereignty to a guru figure. The public started to realize just how dangerous implicit trust of a charismatic guru figure could be. In subsequent decades, as more and more famous gurus got outed as charlatans, frauds, or abusers, the tide really turned against the guru paradigm in the West. Despite this, the cult phenomenon continues, and people continue to be harmed by fraudulent self-appointed gurus.

However, I will still argue that the pendulum of public opinion has swung too far the other way on this issue, leading many people to claim that having a teacher is not necessary on the spiritual path, often proclaiming "I am my own guru" without realizing why that statement is a near enemy of the truth.

When considering this issue, many people are not thinking clearly about the fact that the most famous gurus, with the most followers, the largest operations, and the highest profiles, are precisely the gurus that are most likely to fall from grace. That is because, I argue, most people who amass a huge following very much want to amass a huge following, and the kind of person that wants a huge following is also the kind of person most likely to abuse their charismatic power for personal gain. So, in seeing one famous guru after another fall from grace, most people have made an unfortunate cognitive error: they've decided they can't trust any gurus or spiritual teachers because they're all charlatans. But that's certainly not true. There are countless genuine teachers out there who really do have their students' best interests at heart—people who are teaching out of love for what they do, out of love for the teachings, and out of love for their students. These people are, by and large, not particularly famous. We couldn't even begin to list all the countless teachers who are teaching as an act of service and love and who don't want to take advantage of anyone.* These people aren't seeking adulation; they're

*Having said that, for those readers who are skeptical of my statements here and want real-life examples of awakened teachers with impeccable integrity who are wholly

seeking to share what has been profoundly beneficial for them with others. It's unfortunate, then, that so many people interested in spiritual awakening have largely dismissed the venerable paradigm of studentship—a dismissal often summed up by the phrase "I am my own guru."

Why would I argue that people on the spiritual path need a teacher (or several teachers) for some significant period of their practice? Because I think it happens to be true. Here's why: you can't be your own guru for the same reason that you can't draw a map to a place you've never been. A teacher of spirituality is someone with enough experience to know the terrain of the awakening process and how the practice of meditation helps (and doesn't help) navigate it. The teacher needs to both know the terrain (which includes some potentially dangerous pitfalls, by the way) and be good at mapping it (that is, communicating about it). Such a teacher offers maps that help guide you through the sometimes rough terrain of spiritual awakening. Others have extensive experience but are not good at explaining things, so they're not good teachers. Still others know the theory very well, but don't have enough lived experience to understand the difference between a map and the territory it imperfectly designates (in which case they won't be good at offering alternative maps—that is, alternative perspectives on the same terrain).

You can't draw a map to a place you've never been.

A good teacher is not intrinsically better or more divine than you are. They're just someone with enough experience and communications skills to draw a good map and then explain it well, pointing out in various ways the difference between conceptual map and experiential territory. That's why a teacher is sometimes called in Sanskrit *deśika*, literally "a guide to the territory." If you doubt the need for a

uninterested in self-aggrandizement (despite having become well known, almost in spite of themselves), I will mention four examples out of the many (in the English-speaking world) who come to mind: Adyashanti, Rupert Spira, Jennifer Welwood, and Kavitha Chinnaiyan. Such teachers might seem to lack pizzazz and charisma compared to more famous gurus, but they are infinitely more trustworthy.

guide on at least part of this journey, I suggest that you keep reading. You might find that some of the later sections map territory you have little experience of and wouldn't know to navigate without help.

Now, let's touch on the difference between the teacher-student paradigm and the guru-shishya paradigm. These are, in one sense, the same because the word *guru* just means "teacher" in Sanskrit. Etymologically, it means "one who is heavy with wisdom," a spiritual heavyweight, if you will. In India, if you learn a musical instrument from someone, they are your guru—your harmonium guru or your sitar guru. That language doesn't imply that that person is enlightened; it simply implies they're heavy with knowledge (in this case, musical knowledge); they are a master of their craft. Likewise, *shishya* just means "student," though it can also mean "disciple," which refers to a devoted student who has committed themselves to a particular lineage and its version of spiritual discipline.

Vetting Your Teachers

In the Indian tradition, discipleship is highly regarded, much as apprenticeship used to be a venerated institution in Europe. The healthy version of this paradigm first involves critically examining any teacher of spiritual wisdom for some time (a year is traditionally recommended): questioning them and maintaining healthy skepticism about answers you receive that are not yet verified by your own experience. In reflecting on what you hear from a teacher, you might ask the following questions: Is their teaching coherent yet nondogmatic? Is it sensitive to different types of people without seeking to please everyone? Is it effective? Do people in this teacher's community testify to the efficacy of the practices shared by them?

If you're considering studying and/or practicing with a given teacher in person, it's probably a good idea to interview others who have already done so and ask them about that experience. Of course, someone can be a good teacher even if they don't yet embody everything they teach. A teacher has integrity, I would suggest, if they embody most of what they teach and authentically strive to embody the rest. Spiritual teachers, like their students, are always in a process of integrating the ever-unfolding insights of the spiritual path. No one can accurately claim to have achieved perfect integration, and I would steer clear of anyone who makes that claim (or has others make that claim on their behalf).

After this process of "testing" the teacher, you may decide you can trust this teacher and that there is likely to be spiritual benefit to going deep into studentship with them for a time. If you can trust and open yourself in a relationship with a teacher, you can receive a lot more than if you don't. What you receive in this context is so much more than just information: it's something mysterious that we call transmission. This term refers to something that can flow from an awakened teacher to their student that is more precious than the actual words of the teachings: something like a palpable sense of awakeness, an intuitive glimpse of the paradigm being merely pointed toward by the words. So, in this sense, a shishya is one who has opened to the possibility of transmission.

Now, this paradigm does not require you to believe that your teacher is infallible. You may want to believe your teacher is infallible, and if so you're in a psychologically immature phase (a sometimes necessary phase that I went through), in which you want to believe your teacher never gets anything significant wrong or misreads you in any significant way. But not even a highly intuitive teacher will always give the right teaching at the right moment for you. So, when we talk about trust in the teacher, we're not so much referring to them as a person—the domain of their behavior and conduct—we're referring to trust in the power and efficacy of what they teach and transmit. (Though it's important to note that if any teacher's conduct is sufficiently aberrant that you're not able to open to what they're transmitting, then that's an issue that needs addressing.)

The teachings and practices coming through an authentic teacher are what you seek to open to and trust, but on the personal level, the teacher is not some kind of ideal human that you ought to imitate. They might sometimes be forgetful or neglectful or dismissive in ways that might upset you or even cause some emotional distress. They might not even be a particularly "nice person" in their everyday life. Or they might be wonderfully kind and gentle, but that's not what's important here. That's all on the level of personality, and it's important to separate the office of the teacher from their personality. Their job is to be an effective transmitter of wisdom, a transmitter of the teachings and practices that they have received from their teachers, whereas their personality is just their personality.

The common misapprehension is that if you follow someone's teachings, then you will become like them, in which case their personality and conduct seem terribly important. But authentic teachers are not teaching you something that will make you more like them; they are giving you tools that will make you more like you. They are transmitters of the kind of wisdom that empowers you to become fully what you are.

I would argue that it's a handicap on the path if you regard your teachers as "fully enlightened," since you are then likely to mistake elements of their personality for expressions of enlightenment—and that is definitely not a good idea. It's better if you can see your teacher as a perfectly fallible human being who has seen the kind of truths about existence that are not dependent on the person who's seeing them. Meaning, the universal truths revealed in the awakening process are not contingent on the psychology of the one who sees them. They can't be. And that's why the psychology of the teacher is irrelevant to your awakening.

A Sanskrit text called the Kaula-sūtra says this: "There is but one guru, the unbroken transmission of the shining rays of awakened awareness that are received through the succession of lineage." This means that the guru is not a person but rather the vibration of awakening that can be transmitted through a person—who themselves received it through their teacher (who received it through their teacher, and so on). It can be easy to pedestalize a great teacher because when they are in the zone, as it were, when transmission is flowing through them, they can seem like a luminous beacon of love and light. But that doesn't mean they're like that all the time in everyday life. That luminosity is not a function of who the teacher is as a person; it's a function of the power of transmission, which is very much linked to (but not wholly dependent on) the student's openness and longing to awaken. That's incredibly important to understand. As a shishya, you can trust the transmission, but that doesn't mean you can always trust the teacher as a person. This is at least partially because your perception of them as a person is likely bound up with the psychological phenomenon of projection—at least at first.

There's an old saying in India (almost forgotten today): don't live too close to your guru. That's because one way the mind distracts itself from the awakening process is by focusing on the personhood of the teacher. It's easy to become disillusioned that way, and it's totally missing the point because, again, you're not trying to become like them, you're simply trying to receive the tools and transmission you need to awaken.

Going Against the Grain

Traditionally speaking, sometimes the teacher's job is to challenge you, and if they didn't read you right, that challenge might be off the mark. Or maybe it *was* right on the mark, but you don't like being challenged, so you're likely to resist the teacher's challenge at first and think it's off the mark. Later you might decide "Actually, I think they were saying something I needed to hear; I just didn't want to admit it at the time!" Teachers in the Indian tradition teach in these two kinds of ways, called *anuloma* and *pratiloma* in Sanskrit. The term *anuloma* means "with the grain" or, more literally "with the hair," like petting a cat the right way. *Pratiloma* means "against the grain." Simply put, the former means teaching in a way that's loving, caring, and kind. But in the pratiloma teaching strategy, the teacher appears to be hard on you or is fierce in the way they challenge you, or even teases you (if they perceive you as being too dependent on them, for example). People in the West tend to think that's not appropriate behavior for a teacher, but it is part of the traditional way in Asian culture. It's important to note here that the proof is in the pudding—a fierce teaching strategy is justified only if it's effective in helping you grow and become more centered in your deepest nature, and therefore more free.

So, how do you tell the difference between teaching strategies that beneficially challenge you versus egoic and/or abusive behavior? Look at the results. If the teacher is challenging people in ways that are spiritually effective and not just acting out their own unresolved ego stuff, the results will be obvious. They might try to startle you out of your delusions, push you to be free of magical thinking, or encourage you to examine your motives for practice. Any authentic teacher is always trying to put themselves out of a job, as it were, by helping their students reach the phase of the process where they don't need a teacher—quite the opposite of a charlatan whose mind games seek to bind the student deeper into a codependent relationship.

"You will know them by their fruits," as has been wisely said. We have plenty of examples of teachers who seemed to be trying to use "crazy wisdom" methods but whose communities absolutely imploded in a complete and total shit show.* The testimony of their students is that enormous harm was done.

---

*An obvious example being Andrew Cohen and his EnlightenNext community, which should be a required case study for those who want to understand how even the very best of intentions and visions can go horribly wrong, *little by little*, until a community has become a cult. Cohen's open letter two years after the implosion of his community was equal parts contrite apology and self-defense, so it constitutes

It seems clear to me that if we look at the (admittedly anecdotal) evidence, the number of people who managed to stabilize in the state of awakened awareness without dedicated time with a single teacher (or a group of teachers within the same tradition, offering mutually coherent teachings) is vanishingly small.*

I'm not suggesting here that the reader should go around criticizing those who like to say "I am my own guru." That conceit is only a problem for them if they genuinely want to stabilize in the state of awakened awareness (see page 182). Again, how can you draw a map to a place you've never been? I should note that the process of awakening can begin spontaneously, without the influence of any teacher; here the issue is that of stabilizing in awakened awareness, which is much more rare. A person who wants that must have alignment of view, practice, and fruit (see page 183).

Most teachers offer a piece of the map rather than a whole map of the awakening process. I needed four different teachers in the course of my practice life, each of whom provided a piece of the map, and when those pieces came together, everything finally clicked into place. I needed teachers and never in a million years could have woken up without them, and that's why I feel infinite gratitude to them, their teachers, and their teachers' teachers.

But I've called "I am my own guru" a near enemy, which means it's close to an important truth. In what way? At the end of the day, the buck stops with you. Sure, you need a teacher, or multiple teachers, but the teacher is not a savior. No one can walk the path for you, magically take on your karma, or bestow a magical transmission that pierces through all your veils without any further effort. You have to walk the path—every step of it—yourself. You have to put one foot

---

an interesting example of a former cult leader who acknowledged the harm he caused but didn't fully understand how he caused it (at least, at that time): see andrewcohen.com/open-letter.

*A *stabilized* awakening is one that has become constant, or very nearly so, as the context in which all experience occurs and is furthermore integrated into most aspects of everyday life.

in front of another even when you feel like it's tearing you apart and you can't go on. There are other moments, of course, when you're walking on sunshine and you think, "Okay, I'm out of the woods now, and it's all golden forever!" Then the next week or next month, it's back to "I don't know how I can go on another step!" But you have to. Nobody else can do it for you.

The teacher orients you in the right direction, which is crucial. If you're faced in the wrong direction, it doesn't matter whether you're a star athlete or you're dragging your feet. But though the orientation and inspiration our teachers give us is indispensable for most, the journey is still uniquely yours, which is why a good teacher will say, "Don't give your power away to me. Don't abdicate responsibility. I'm showing you signposts and pointing out pitfalls and making recommendations, but it's up to you to think for yourself and decide which of these is relevant to you."

You are never exempt from the need for discernment. No matter how much you love your teacher, no matter how full of wisdom you think they are, never give your power away or relinquish your discernment. The buck stops with you.

NEAR ENEMY #15

All Paths Lead to the Same Goal

THERE'S A FORM of seemingly benign wishful thinking expressed in a cliché found in many alternative spiritual communities: "All paths lead to the same goal." This idea is often strongly linked to the popular notion that all religions are fundamentally talking about the same thing. One can only believe the latter statement through an extreme version of the logical fallacy called cherry-picking, and one can only believe the former by not looking too closely at the true diversity of spiritual traditions and their professed goals.

The Goal of Liberation

In South Asian traditions, the single word that's most often used to name the goal of the spiritual path is *liberation* (*mokṣa* or *mukti* in Sanskrit, though we also see terms like *paramārtha,* "ultimate reality," and *bodhi,* "awakened awareness"). The frequent recurrence of the word *liberation* to designate the goal in different systems of practice implies to the casual reader that the same goal is being posited. However, when one investigates what liberation means in these different systems, one finds very different answers. Here are some of the diverse spiritual goals to which the word *liberation* can refer in the South Asian context:

- The end of suffering
- Escape from saṁsāra (the otherwise endless cycle of death and rebirth)
- The complete cessation of the desire for anything to be other than as it is (nirvāṇa)
- Final separation from the inherently flawed material universe (kaivalya)
- The manifestation of one's innate divinity (*śivatva-abhivyakti*), either at the time of death or in this very body (the latter possibility being called jīvanmukti)
- Unity-consciousness (*aikātmya*)
- Immersion in the ocean of pure being (*samāveśa*)
- A state of pure contentless consciousness, totally withdrawn from the world (samādhi)
- Dissolution of the conditioned mind (*citta-laya*)
- Attainment of a heavenly realm where one experiences eternal communion with a separate and superior God
- Becoming equal to God in all respects (omniscient, omnipotent, etc.) but still separate from Him
- Becoming one with the Absolute
- Realizing your already-existent oneness with the Absolute
- Realization of the emptiness of all phenomena
- And many more

Let's explore some of these a bit further. In the first instance, liberation means a definitive exit from saṁsāra—that is, an escape from the cycle of death and rebirth. In ancient times (more than two thousand years ago), this was the commonest definition of *liberation.* This is not a goal that modern people tend to relate to. I've heard many say, "What's wrong with reincarnation? Life is beautiful. Why would I want to stop being born again and again?" Of course, I've only heard this question from privileged individuals in highly developed nations. Most humans throughout most of recorded history have had unremittingly hard lives, and when faced with a choice between playing that tragic tune on repeat ad infinitum and any other option, choosing the latter is at the very least understandable—even though when this notion was first posited, there was no indication in the literature of what escape from saṁsāra would experientially entail. Nonexistence, or some nonearthly existence? For the early yogis, it didn't matter. They just wanted to transcend this world.

For the classical Yoga tradition, exemplified by the Yoga-sūtra of Patañjali, the goal of the spiritual path is permanently disentangling oneself from the inherently flawed material universe (the state known as kaivalya). This is similar to the previously described goal except here, one definitively continues to exist as pure soul—that is to say, as pure contentless consciousness, contentedly free of all experience whatsoever.

Various Views of Selfhood

By contrast, some Buddhist lineages (and some Advaita lineages as well) believe that the primary goal of the spiritual path is best articulated as the dissolution of the illusion of selfhood. We could also call it the annihilation of ego: the end of the story of "me," which turns out to have been nothing but a mental construct all along. One realizes that "I" is nothing but a thought, and therefore, self-referencing (also known as taking things personally) is a kind of imaginary activity, one that causes considerable needless suffering.

Most people who undergo this kind of ego dissolution experience it as a fairly cataclysmic event, but others don't. For some, after years of mindfulness meditation, the sense of separate self just slips away and doesn't come back. By contrast, those who suddenly find themselves on the brink of the cessation of selfhood are nearly always convinced that they are literally going to die. It's a fascinating fact that the constructed selfhood of the psyche is so strong, so firmly reified, that when it's on the verge of shearing apart, the person often feels that that they couldn't possibly survive the process. It can feel like impending death or that one is about to go mad, but paradoxically, by surrendering to the process, neither occurs. Such feeling-thoughts turn out to be the last-ditch defenses of the illusory self.

But if that's not your cup of tea, some Hindu traditions articulate a completely different version of the goal: unity-consciousness of one variety or another. This is the state of feeling absolutely one with everything while still possessing a self. The self has become all-inclusive. People often glimpse this state on psychedelics and "plant medicines," and it can be a wonderful experience. But there is also a pitfall here: when this state is co-opted by the ego, one can develop delusions of grandeur. We've seen several prominent gurus fall victim to this pitfall, so it's not to be taken lightly. But if the pitfall can be avoided, unity-consciousness can stabilize into a state in which joy is a nearly constant by-product (this is sometimes called *cidānanda,* the joy of awareness, in Sanskrit).

It is also possible to experience something closely adjacent to unity-consciousness, something we might call abiding nondual awareness. In this paradigm, there's not so much a feeling of being one with everything but rather of everything being simply "one, without a second." There's no self that experiences oneness nor is there specifically an absence of self; there's just consciousness manifesting as the ever-changing mass of phenomena, including, at times, that which seems like a self (but is seen to be just another appearance within consciousness, like everything else).

Some dualistic South Asian traditions, such as the Gauḍiya Vaishnavas (popularly known as the Hare Krishnas), believe liberation constitutes winning the grace of Lord Krishna (seen as the one and only Godhead) through devotion to Him and thereby attaining His heavenly realm after death, a realm where one eternally sports in His divine company in the most exquisitely beautiful pastoral-cum-celestial setting imaginable. There's no merging with God on this view. That's not the goal of the path. This version of ultimate spiritual beatitude is conceptually almost identical to the goal of Christianity, though of course the aesthetic imagery is different.

Some readers will imagine that Buddhism, seen in the West as an intellectually sophisticated atheistic religion, couldn't possibly have a parallel to the goal described in the previous paragraph. But it does: Pure Land Buddhism, popular in East Asia, is virtually identical to the form of Vaishnavism just described (theologically, not aesthetically). Here Amitābha Buddha has taken the place of Krishna, but again the goal is to attain a paradisical heavenly realm where He resides, and the primary method of doing so is through devotion to Him enacted through repeating His mantra.

I hope you're beginning to concede that these religious traditions have radically different goals. But let's touch on a couple of more.

Becoming Godlike and Attaining Personal Power

The culmination of spiritual practice according to some Shaivite traditions is to become Godlike. On this view, one can attain exactly the same powers and abilities of Shiva, who is seen as the creator, sustainer, and destroyer of the whole universe. You are said to manifest the potential of your "Shiva-equal soul" at liberation and thereby become omniscient and omnipotent. However, out of respect to the "original Shiva," you don't go about creating and destroying worlds; you just enjoy being Godlike, being God's equal. But you don't even hang out together. You're separate but equal.

Finally, a few practitioners in any of several South Asian religious traditions seek a goal of purely personal power. They want to master the eight magical powers (at a minimum), which in this religious imaginarium would make one the equal of half-a-dozen Marvel superheroes combined.* Historically, such yogis did not necessarily seek power to do good: they often sought to master aggressive magical rites (or "black magic") as well as supernatural powers that could be used in any manner. Their version of liberation was that attained through total personal power.

Clearly, all these descriptions of the goal of the spiritual life are quite different. Pondering them, it's hard to imagine how people came up with the idea that "All paths lead to the same goal" in the first place. In the scholarly book *Roots of Yoga,* my colleague Dr. James Mallinson writes:

> This rather bewildering array of ideas about liberation suggests an interesting counterpoint to a particular perspective on (Indian) spirituality that is characteristic of perennial philosophy and the New Age. This view, which holds considerable currency in contemporary globalized yoga, proposes that the paths to the ultimate goal are many, while the goal itself is one, and common to all the world's religious and spiritual traditions. However, what we see . . . is that even in the (relatively) limited context of Indian religion, the goals are also many. Indeed, restricting the argument to

*The eight traditional magical powers include the ability to become minute (like Ant-Man), weightless and fly, and incredibly dense and heavy, as well as to magically manifest anything you like, control and manipulate any person or element, etc.

> the history of Indian yoga, we might further venture that, with the consolidation of *haṭha*-inflected eightfold yoga as a shared technique across a variety of metaphysical and doctrinal traditions from the seventeenth century, we see a situation in which one path leads to many goals.*

I think Dr. Mallinson is mostly correct here, but I might quibble with his last sentence, in which he's speaking from the point of view of his specialty, which is the study of the way Yoga was practiced just before colonialism, in the early modern period (the sixteenth through the early eighteenth centuries). He's saying that what he's seeing in his sources is that many practitioners in the early modern period are using the same Yoga techniques, which have become sort of standardized, but still articulating different goals. However, in the early medieval period in which I specialize (the eight through eleventh centuries), we see significantly different forms of practice that are calibrated more precisely to those different goals. There's a far greater variety of practices prior to the consolidation into the monolith of Hinduism (which began in the fourteenth or fifteenth century).

But again, we return to the crucial question: How is "All paths lead to the same goal" a near enemy of the truth? In reality, the bullet-point list I presented earlier is overly simplistic because these various goals cannot be considered mutually exclusive in any cut-and-dried way. In truth, many of them overlap in various complex ways. For example, a given sect could acknowledge the goals of other sects as progressive but subordinate stages on its own path (we see this hermeneutic strategy especially clearly in the tradition of nondual Shaiva Tantra, which I study).**

*James Mallinson and Mark Singleton, *Roots of Yoga* (New York: Penguin Books, 2017), 396.

**See for example, chapter 8 of *The Recognition Sutras*.

Awakening

If we focus particularly on those spiritual traditions in which the word *yoga* was a central term of discourse, we find much more overlap in the descriptions of the goal of spiritual practice, such that they can all be subsumed under the headings of just two words: *bodha* and *mokṣa*, where the first term means "awakening to your true nature" or "becoming aware of what is most fundamentally true about your own being," and the second term means "becoming free of the egoic self and the limitations on experience it imposes, and further becoming free of all mind-created suffering." These statements about the goal of practice would be intelligible to nearly all practitioners of the yogic arts (aside from the power seekers). In other words, almost all the traditions for whom the word *yoga* is a central term believe and testify that the practice will lead to permanent liberation from the majority of suffering, ego, and self-limitation and a concomitant immersion into what is fundamentally true.

The theme of awakening and liberation as two sides of one coin is found in a Tantric text, the Mṛgendra-tantra, which describes the goal in these words:

> He experiences the unfolding of his own nature as all-encompassing vision and [unhindered] action, full of bliss and eternal. Once he has attained this [realization], he is never touched again by the suffering that perpetuates the pernicious [condition of transmigratory existence].*

Many, perhaps even all, of the Tantric traditions would agree with that articulation of the goal, but they disagree sometimes about whether you can achieve it in this very body as opposed to achieving it in a postulated after-death state—so that obviously constitutes a

*Translated by Alexis Sanderson in The Yoga Section of the Mṛgendratantra (27), oxford.academia.edu/AlexisSanderson.

significant difference. But my argument here is that Mallinson's quote significantly overstates the case, at least with respect to the period in which Tantric Yoga flourished. The goal of spiritual practice, for the countless lineages that fall under the rubric of classical Tantra (and for many that don't as well), is awakening to our true nature (bodha) and shifting into a paradigm of radical freedom (mokṣa). Many of the goals in the bullet-point list (see page 160) can be subsumed under these two words, apart from the strictly dualistic ones. The bullet-point list serves to represent the fact that a lot of ink was spilled over the centuries on how exactly to define and describe this twofold goal in words, but those discussions are mostly of interest to academics and philosophers. For most practitioners, virtually any version of bodha and mokṣa constitutes a deep and extraordinary fulfillment of practice.

So, the extent to which the statement "All paths lead to the same goal" is wrong depends on how wide your lens is—that is to say, the degree of variety of cultures and spiritual traditions you're looking at. But let's talk about where the rubber meets the road on this issue. If it were true that all paths lead to the same goal, it wouldn't matter which path you choose. But if this platitude is closer to not-true than it is to true, as I'm arguing here, then it matters very much which path you choose—but not necessarily for the reasons you might think.

View, Practice, and Fruit

The Tantric tradition discusses this issue in terms of the concept of alignment of view, practice, and fruit, where the first term refers to the philosophy you embrace and the third term refers to the goal of practice. It teaches that alignment of these three elements is necessary for the spiritual path to work. So, to put it simply, first you need to ensure that you are cultivating a view (studying a spiritual philosophy) that aligns with your practice (i.e., that supports it and is fully compatible with it). Second, you need to ensure that your practices align with what you are seeking to actualize—your goal. To put it another way, you should consider whether you have good reasons to believe that your practices are likely to actualize your goal.

Without the alignment of view, practice, and fruit, the spiritual path doesn't accomplish anything of substance. For many people, that doesn't really matter, since spirituality is basically a hobby for them, even if they wouldn't say so. Others are serious about the spiritual path and are just lucky enough to stumble onto a version of it in which view, practice, and fruit are already aligned. Such practitioners might then actualize the goal without ever pondering the importance of such alignment. But most practitioners, I would say, need to consider this issue and try to make sure they have this alignment.

Even if you've already been practicing for many years, checking your alignment can be a profoundly beneficial contemplation. I suggest that you start with a deep and careful contemplation of your goal. Why are you really doing any of this spiritual stuff? What is your heart's deepest longing in this domain? The modern spiritual teacher Adyashanti writes about this beautifully and clearly in his book *The Way of Liberation.** To clarify your aspiration, you need to get quite specific. Vague spiritual-sounding language that simply parrots what you've heard is insufficient.** Some offer a cop-out at this point, essentially saying that having a goal is itself unspiritual. This is self-deceptive nonsense, I argue. Nobody engages any time-consuming project without the idea that a desirable outcome of some kind is possible. So, this contemplation is a matter of making that implicit desire explicit and bringing it into clear focus.

---

*This discussion can be found under the heading "Clarify Your Aspiration" (page 3). *The Way of Liberation* is of interest to a scholar-practitioner like myself because it's the author's attempt to capture the minimum amount of information and guidance that is necessary and sufficient to successfully walk the spiritual path.

**There's an amusing and instructive satire of such language at the beginning of Jed McKenna's first book, *Spiritual Enlightenment, the Damnedest Thing* (Wisefool Press, 2011)

Having clarified your aspiration, you then ask yourself, and your teachers, "Are the practices I'm doing likely to actualize the goal that I'm oriented toward?" Even though it's impossible to be absolutely sure about the answer to that question, I recommend asking it of yourself and whoever you think is wise in this domain. Let's consider a simple example to clarify this issue of alignment. Most of the practices taught in modern yoga studios are oriented to the goals of health and well-being, not the goals of awakening and liberation (this despite the fact the fact that the latter tend to result in the maximum well-being possible for a given person). If your goal is some version of awakening and liberation (and remember, it needs to be defined more specifically than that, in terms meaningful to you), then it's good to know that the practices offered in modern yoga are out of alignment with that goal, either in the sense that they are simply insufficient or that they may even be counterproductive with respect to that goal. (For example, if competition and physical performance is emphasized in the culture of a given yoga studio, that tends to exacerbate mental states that are hindrances to awakening and liberation.)

The final step in this process is to inquire into whether the spiritual philosophy that you're working with (also known as view) is sufficiently aligned with the type of practice that you're doing. It turns out that this really matters. The understanding you bring to spiritual practice can undermine or greatly enhance the impact of that practice. For example, modern yoga sometimes teaches "purification" practices of mind and body that in some cases are incompatible with a nondual view. These practices arose in the context of dualistic forms of yoga that regarded the body as inherently impure and spiritually problematic even in its normal, healthy state. On a subtler level, practices that consistently privilege transcendental or altered states of consciousness over and against so-called ordinary states of consciousness are incompatible with a nondual view. And if they are incompatible with a given view, then they are necessarily also incompatible with the goal taught by that view. How could one whose practice implicitly glorifies certain states of consciousness over others enter into all-embracing nondual awareness? In this way, without contemplation, we easily end up working at cross-purposes with our own intention and spinning our wheels, as it were.

Of course, the easiest way to ensure compatibility of view and practice is to practice exclusively within a specific tradition in which they both evolved together over centuries, informing each other. Many people today are averse to this idea of a traditional practice, but like it or not, most modern yoga studios and eclectic spiritual centers operating within the capitalist model give no thought to this issue of compatibility because they can't afford to (or so the owners tend to believe). Therefore, it's common to hear spiritual teachings peppered into modern yoga classes that are both superficial and incompatible with the form of practice being taught. "Love yourself just as you are" but also "Drop those extra pounds! Sculpt that butt!" or "Be the best version of yourself!" or "Purify your mind of negative thoughts, and let go of negative emotions." How can a practice in which one is constantly attempting to manipulate and control one's experience lead to a state in which one relaxes into one's innate state of freedom and thereby falls in love with the whole pattern of reality? It can't. Not in a million years.

The understanding you bring to spiritual practice can undermine or greatly enhance the impact of that practice.

Once you have alignment of view, practice, and fruit, the spiritual life takes off. It's like you were in an old jalopy and suddenly you're in a Maserati. Or, perhaps a better metaphor, you've been spinning your wheels and now they touch down. This alignment gives you real traction. The difference is unmistakable.

CONTEMPLATIVE EXERCISE

Clarify Your Aspiration

Having set aside some quiet time, sit down with your journal or notebook. Get settled and ask yourself this question: What am I seeking to actualize with my spiritual practice? What do I want? What result do I envision? In this contemplation, answers like "enlightenment" or "liberation" are unacceptable unless you know exactly what you mean by those words. Don't just parrot what you've heard. Rather, see if you can write a sentence or two about precisely what you are seeking to actualize through your practice. Ideally, it's something that you've had an experiential taste of and would like to realize and embody more fully. On the other hand, if your most authentic answer is "I want to realize what's most deeply true, regardless of what that is," that is an acceptable answer as well since the aspiration for truth can arise organically for some people. Note that you might revise this articulation of your aspiration every few months as you get more and more clear, through direct experience, about where the spiritual path can lead (and where it can't).

NEAR ENEMIES #16 & 17

The Universe Is Giving Me a Sign and Go With the Flow

HERE I'VE COMBINED two near enemies because they are intimately related, as we shall see. First, let's acknowledge that many popular authors use the phrase "the Universe" exactly as other people use the word "God." For example, self-help guru Jack Canfield says, "The Universe works in mysterious ways. It is constantly working to make available to you the tools, the resources, the people and the lessons you need to become the person you were meant to be." Clearly, in Canfield's view, the Universe has a plan for you. This is, of course, sheerest nonsense. The universe is not a person. It doesn't make plans for us or try to teach us lessons. The universe is simply a collective term for the totality of phenomena, and the language used by Canfield, Abraham Hicks, and others is merely a reinvented version of contemporary Christian theology for people mildly allergic to the word God.

If the universe doesn't send you messages, give you signs, or teach you lessons, then how is this not a far enemy rather than a near one? I've suggested in previous chapters that the reality in which we live is not random but patterned. I would even say, on the basis of both direct spiritual insight and the tradition in which I've trained, that the pattern of reality exhibits extraordinary intelligence. But I do not go so far as to claim that that intelligence belongs to a person, a putative superhuman God. A pattern can exhibit what we may call intelligence, in the sense of being precisely calibrated and finely balanced, without suggesting that someone designed it that way. For example, the universe in which we live is fine-tuned for life,* certainly, but it may be that there are countless universes, in which case of course we live in the one among millions that is capable of producing life.

Having noted that the pattern of reality is intelligent (for lack of a better term), we can even suggest that it 'supports' the process of spiritual awakening, not because of a mystical plan made by a superhuman being to help us awaken, but rather because awakening is simply becoming more attuned to the nature of reality. Since reality is as it is, it's only logical that the process of attuning to it will appear to be 'supported' by it, since misunderstandings of the nature of reality will be incompatible with that process of attunement, to the precise degree that they are misunderstandings.

What makes this process mysterious is simply the fact that our conscious minds are far from capable of tracking the countless factors in play in the arising of any given experience. That is to say, the

---

*As Stephen Hawking has noted, «The laws of science, as we know them at present, contain many fundamental numbers, like the size of the electric charge of the electron and the ratio of the masses of the proton and the electron. . . . The remarkable fact is that the values of these numbers seem to have been very finely adjusted to make possible the development of life.» If, for example, the strong nuclear force were 1% stronger or weaker than it is, this would drastically alter the physics of stars, and probably preclude the existence of life similar to what we observe on Earth. (en.wikipedia.org/wiki/Fine-tuned_universe)

pattern that produces experience, and causes it to have the character that it does, is far too complex and subtle for us to parse it with our conscious minds. Therefore, the synchronicities we notice when we are in the process of attuning to the nature of reality can appear to be positively magical. But it is far too easy to attribute too much significance to these synchronicities and interpret them as a "sign from the universe," when in fact synchronicities are simply the norm when we're becoming more aware of the pattern of reality.

My root-teacher used to say, "If something comes to your attention, it deserves your attention" and this is a much more useful formulation than "The universe is sending me a sign." Sometimes we notice something that barely registers because the volume of the thinking mind is so dominant, but that subtle noticing could be the operation of the adaptive unconscious (as some cognitive scientists refer to what most people call the 'subconscious mind') seeking to alert the conscious mind to something it might be beneficial to be aware of. When the volume of the prattling mind or 'inner narrator' is turned down through meditation, such noticing, and the intuitive response to what is noticed, become much more clear.

Through attentiveness to our total environment (including the body) rather than the compulsively thinking mind, we pick up all sorts of cues that we might otherwise miss. These cues may not be understood by the conscious mind, but they can still feed into the intelligent matrix of the adaptive unconscious effectively. Therefore, we don't need to wonder "What does it mean?"—we can simply be calmly attentive and aware, and trust the intuitions that organically arise in the wake of such attentiveness.

Here I'm describing the commonest state of affairs—but it can happen, on rare occassions, that something truly extraordinary occurs, something that seems hard to consider as anything other than a "sign from the universe." Like that time you were praying for guidance, feeling at the end of your rope, and that same day you found a spiritual book randomly left behind in a public place that gave you just the guidance you needed. Or some similar incident. If the universe isn't a person who sends us messages, how do we explain such an incident? A skeptical observer will just call it coincidence, but for the person to whom it happens it feels far too meaningful to dismiss it in that way. Though I don't have a definitive explanation to offer, I have seen it happen time and time again that when the longing for awakening is strong, it seems as if the pattern of reality organizes itself to support it. It may be that the sounder explanation is a form of confirmation bias—that one is simply better at noticing that which might support the spiritual journey when one's focus is strongly on the latter. But this does not explain those incidents when something falls into one's lap that doesn't immediately seem relevant but proves so subsequently.

In all cases, whether the apparent sign is subtle or dramatic, my recommendation is to gently turn away from the mind's compulsion to assign an imagined meaning to the incident right away, and rather get quiet inside and listen for the wordless intuitive prompt that arises in the wake of the apparent sign (if any). If the incident does have significance, then it will certainly facilitate such an intuitive prompt.

Many people interpret the injunction to "go with the flow" in a manner similar to "the universe is giving me a sign." In this view, if you're on your way somewhere and you run into an obstacle, you should consider turning back or going somewhere else, because clearly your original plan is "not in the flow." Likewise, if you get a tummy-ache when contemplating that evening's plans, you should cancel the plans. These 'signs' are taken to indicate what is and isn't in the flow. Someone who interprets "go with the flow" in this superficial way, however, will act impulsively upon passing whims, and will always tend to prioritize their needs over those of others, though a mountain of psychological studies have shown us that this is not a good strategy for long-term happiness in life.*

Nonetheless, I would suggest, though I cannot prove, that there is a natural flow to the pattern of existence. Or rather, that the pattern is made up of countless currents of flow, many of which intersect with and influence our primary life-current, as it were. Furthermore, I would suggest that we all sense these currents in some way, however slightly. We resist them when our cultural conditioning predisposes us to do so, as when we cling to a job (or a marriage) for the financial security it provides even though we feel the current of life taking us in another direction. Resisting these currents only causes us suffering, for life will always have its way with us sooner or later. If we resist too long, we may be brought to a crisis point, which generally entails an extra dose of suffering. By contrast, there is a unique joy in merging with the natural currents of life. A sense of ineffable rightness. And if flowing with the natural currents of life becomes your default state, after some time it becomes impossible to imagine doing otherwise.

Here we must distinguish between the shallow currents and the deep ones. The shallow ones are more noticeable, oftentimes, but less consequential (usually). An example might be the pull to take your holiday here instead of there, in contrast to a deep current which pulls you away from a job or long-term relationship, or towards a spiritual retreat, or compels you to move to another country. But it would be too easy to define deep currents in terms of the perceived significance of the decision they pull you towards. Rather, they share these defining features: they are quieter, subtler, yet more powerful and inexorable than the shallow currents. And you might feel them many months or even years before they translate into observable events. For example, I started feeling the pull to move to Portugal, a country which I had never even visited, more than two

---

* See, among others, *The Happiness Hypothesis* by Jonathan Haidt.

years before it happened. There was no priming involved (that is, no one suggested it to me) and no sign of how it might happen. But it did, and now I live in an old stone cottage in the middle of nowhere in central Portugal (perfect for a writer), with my small retreat center nearby.

By the same token, we must distinguish shallow currents from the whims of the mind. Though the shallow currents are less powerful and less consequential than the deep ones, they are still currents of life-energy, and so are distinct from the phenomenon of the mind flitting here and there with thoughts of "Maybe I should . . ." In general, it's safe to say the mind's grasping at straws with thoughts of "maybe I should do this or that" can be ignored, because if any of those ideas actually line up with the natural currents of life-energy, then that will become clear in time as you start to sense the slow wordless pull of a new current. This 'pull' to which I refer is exactly that which was discussed in several earlier chapters under the name pratibhā.

In this paradigm, little by little you learn to want whatever Life wants. This is not some passive state of resignation, but quite the opposite: a curious eagerness to discover where the currents of life-energy are flowing and the active desire to merge with them, rather than holding yourself separate and apart. The good news is, when you want what Life wants, you'll always get what you want.*

Signs and Synchronicities

As is the case with several other near enemies, the near enemy of "go with the flow" is merely the facile and superficial interpretation of that phrase. When you learn to go with the flow of life's currents, you won't need "signs from the universe" to point out your direction;

*This phrase comes from my former teacher Adyashanti, specifically the talk entitled "True Manifesting," which I highly recommend.

rather, such 'signs' and synchronicities arise as mere confirmations that you are, indeed, in the flow. But a caveat applies here: in certain hyper-activated mental states, people imagine they see signs that would not be considered such in a more sober frame of mind. Sometimes the desire to see signs everywhere is motivated by the dopamine hit such imagined seeing confers. For example, it really doesn't mean anything if you look at the clock every time it's 11:11 (as a current trend seems to insist). For one thing, time is a mental construct, so there's no significance to any numbers on the clock, and for another, if you are super-motivated to keep seeing those numbers, your subconscious will cue you when to look at the phone so you can see them and get your dopamine hit. Synchronicities don't demonstrate that you have a special connection to "Source Energy" as some people claim. They don't demonstrate anything at all, unless the synchronicity brings your attention to something that, when soberly contemplated, reveals an insight that remains insightful the following day (or week, or month). Perhaps an apparent 'sign' makes you aware of a current that is slowly gathering force and that will take you in a different direction in life. But 'signs' and synchronicities that get you excited but don't reveal anything are not indicative of anything save your addiction to excitement.

Of course, here we must distinguish between the sometimes slow, and always 'organic,' revelation of significance and the mind's compulsive assignation of imagined meaning. The former is wordless; the sense of significance is there prior to any mental interpretation of it. It reveals itself organically, like a new bud sprouting from the fertile soil of nonconceptual contemplation. By contrast, the mind's compulsive assignation of imagined meaning is quick and exciting but fades rapidly and doesn't actually connect us to a deeper sense of being.

To verify for yourself everything I've said in this chapter, meditation is almost certainly necessary. Through meditation, the chatter of the mind eventually quiets down and we become able to palpably sense the currents of life-energy referred to above. Through meditation, we relax our compulsions and become less attached to the emotional hits of excitement that come with imagined revelations. We become serenely sober, in which state clear seeing is possible. Though many of my students consider me an expert guide to the art of meditation, I know of no better introduction to meditation than Adyashanti's book (and audiobook) *True Meditation*. How you learn the art of meditation is of great consequence because performed incorrectly, meditation can actually strengthen the ego-self and keep you stuck in a rut; and performed correctly, as a non-manipulative act in the way Adyashanti describes, it can be the greatest possible ally on the journey of awakening. It helps us perceive in a manner free from the mind's compulsions, confabulations, and unwarranted leaps.

As Barks' Rumi says, "Let yourself be silently drawn by the strange pull of what you really love. It will not lead you astray." May you merge with the natural currents of your life, and go with the flow in the deepest possible sense. May you be free of the mental compulsion to project your desires and values onto the universe at large, and learn to listen rather than impute. And may you experience the sweet joy of co-creatively dancing with the pattern of reality, flowing with its currents rather than resisting them.

CONTEMPLATIVE EXERCISE

The Currents of Life

Take several deep breaths; breathe as many long and slow breaths as it takes until you feel settled. When settled, give your awareness to your total life situation, without adding any judgements or verbal thoughts on top of it. As you situate yourself in this juncture in time, in your total life situation, become aware of any 'currents' that are already flowing but that you haven't given attention to. It may help to ask yourself "What do I already know to be true that I'm not admitting to myself?" You're not looking for an answer in words, though words may form subsequently to describe what you sense. You're just looking to become more aware of what already is in the realm of perception beyond the five senses. Awareness of that realm comes slowly. Be open, and patient.

PART TWO

FINDING DEEPER CURRENTS

Reality

WHILE WRITING THIS BOOK, it struck me that even single words representing complex or subtle concepts, words like *reality, enlightenment,* and *ego,* can be near enemies, in the sense that the interpretations that they are commonly given constitute near enemies of the truth to which those words might more usefully point. In this section of the book, I focus on how these words have been understood in less-than-beneficial ways and how we might understand them in much more beneficial ways on the spiritual path.

The nature of reality is a central issue on the spiritual path. South Asian traditions call the question of the nature of reality paramārtha, the domain of ultimate truth. Here I argue that the confounding problem in this domain is the human mind's tendency to confuse what is with our *mental representations* of what is. I will distinguish these two with the phrases "first-order reality" and "second-order reality." I believe those labels are more useful than the tendency some nondualist teachers have to label the domain of second-order reality—thoughts, memories, imagination, etc.—as "unreal."

First-order reality may be defined as what we experience before we have a thought about it or an interpretation of it. Second-order reality is constituted by our interpretations, stories, narratives, or mental frames: ways that we represent our experience to ourselves and to others. Anything that we can put into words is automatically second-order reality. It's a representation of our direct experience.

Another way to say this is that first-order reality is what presents, and second-order reality is our mental re-presentation of what presents. First-order reality includes not only sensual perceptions, but also all sorts of sensations (including the sensations we label "emotions"), as well as instinctive desires and needs (ones that don't arise on the basis of a thought).

Though this distinction seems obvious when described in this way, in practice it can be difficult for human beings to grasp. People constantly confuse their narratives about reality with reality itself. To parse this difference experientially, most people need some substantial experience in meditation. This is because meditation has, for many, the effect of slightly widening the gap between direct experience and interpretation. It can also facilitate the ability to rest in not knowing; that is to say, on the basis of a meditation practice, the compulsion to form a narrative before one has enough information to make a plausible and useful one arises less and less often. Furthermore, one learns to enjoy the state of not knowing, whereas for most nonmeditators it causes anxiety.

It seems to me that some values can also be a part of first-order reality. Some things matter to you more than others prior to any thought or interpretation. You might experience an emotion, and that might be linked to a need that is intrinsic to our human nature, such as the need for human connection. But through a process of spiritual or psychological maturation, the edginess or urgency of that need might fall away, and then we can say that you value connection rather than need it.

So, emotions, needs, and values can be part of first-order reality. You can experience a sweet (or desperate) longing for connection even before you have a thought about it. It's natural, not a product of cultural conditioning (which means deeply internalized thoughts and narratives). There's a wide range of emotions that can exist before you have a thought about them, but it's also the case that as soon as you label the emotion, it changes your relationship to it. Emotions are nothing but interpreted physiological sensations, and some emotions are judged as negative or problematic, such as anxiety, even though anxiety is physiologically indistinguishable from certain types of excitement, which we do not judge as negative or problematic.

So, these elements of first-order reality we call emotions might be reinforced by thought, justified by thought, or interpreted by thought. And it's also the case that there are certain emotions that exist only because of certain thoughts. They are generated by believing thoughts. An easy example would be envy or jealousy—they only arise on the basis of thinking about a situation in a particular way and believing those thoughts. Some versions of depression are also caused by believing certain thoughts. I would suggest that these are precisely the kinds of states and emotions that fall away when we're far enough along the spectrum of awakening.

A central feature of what we mean by awakeness, then, is the ability to distinguish between first-order and second-order reality. But this teaching does not amount to saying that second-order reality is invalid. Our representations and interpretations of our experience are perfectly real as representations. They can never capture the totality, nuance, complexity, or subtlety of our experience, but nonetheless, they have their own reality and their own power.

A Spiritual Cul-de Sac

There are some spiritual teachers out there who doggedly work to help people get free from their stories, or at least from their emotional attachment to their stories. This is a perfectly valid and important part of the spiritual enterprise. But it can also lead to a spiritual cul-de-sac, where we discount and dismiss other peoples' interpretations of their experience without being sufficiently curious about the experiences that gave rise to those interpretations.

The ability to distinguish between first-order and second-order reality, between experience and interpretation, doesn't require us to entirely invalidate those interpretations; it only requires us to see them for what they are. When we look into this matter, we discover that not every interpretation is equally contingent on the experience that it purports to interpret. Most are contingent on much more than that—namely, our history, psychology, and cultural conditioning. The latter comes to us through parents, teachers, friends, social media, movies, and television—all these influences form the conditioning that partially determines how we interpret any given experience. Even more so, our unresolved painful or pleasurable past experiences influence how we interpret any given present-moment experience. An inability to see this fact clearly in emotionally charged moments, and compensate for it to some degree, makes interpersonal relationships very difficult, to say the least.

The reason why some spiritual teachers say "Thoughts are not true" is that they're trying to get across that second-order reality is not first-order reality. And indeed it can be a mind-blowing realization to discover that you are not your story about yourself, and everyone in your life is not your story about them. Even when you have very strong, emotionally charged, and thoroughly fleshed-out stories, the person that they're about is still not your story about them. They are not reducible to your diagnosis or mental picture of them. Which is not to say that your story has no value or that it has no relationship to reality. The teaching here is simply this: if you confuse first- and second-order reality, then by definition you're asleep. You're not noticing that the dream is a dream. That's the opposite of awakeness. Of course, we can be awake in some dimensions of our lives and asleep in others. Whenever you act as though your story about someone is a true description of them, rather than a psychologically contingent description of your experience of them, this is confusing first- and second-order reality. On the other hand, there's a form of spiritual bypassing that can happen when we discount our own or someone else's story. Spiritual folks are fond of saying "That's just a story"—but perhaps the story points to, or is a clumsy attempt to point to, real aspects of the other person's experience with you that merit addressing.

It can be a mind-blowing realization to discover that you are not your story about yourself.

A wonderful part of awakeness is the ability to repose in the embodied (that is to say, visceral) awareness that you are not your story about yourself or anybody else's story about you. If you really get that, then you don't jump to defend or justify yourself and discount their story. It's only when you're still trying to get yourself to believe that you're not their story about you that you bother to discount it. When you know that you're not their story about you, then you can listen to what they're sharing about their experience with you, even if they're expressing it in judgmental terms. Their image of you might not fit your image of yourself, but that's not the point—their story is true insofar as it points to genuine aspects of their lived experience in relationship to you, however distorted by their inability to parse first- and second-order reality.

Cognitive Bias

The word *story* is useful in this teaching because we can all understand that fictional stories we find compelling tell us something true about human experience. It's the same with our narratives about interpersonal experiences. If you wrote up an analysis of yourself, or of someone else, it's likely that nearly every single sentence of that analysis would connect to your lived experience in some way. But that doesn't make it true as stated. Indeed, it's inevitably distorted in countless ways, such as in its attribution of causes or apportionment of blame. A story, interpretation, or narrative is inevitably a distortion because it's necessarily partial and fragmentary. You can never tell the complete story because accounting for every single impinging factor and every single nuance of experience is simply impossible.

Since you can't tell a complete story, somebody else who witnessed the same events would tell a different story about it because they're choosing different fragments of experience to focus on, unconsciously based on their experience and cognitive biases. Indeed, it's almost certainly the case that even if two people try to objectively remember everything they can about a series of events both were present for, they will still remember some different things. But the deeper issue is that when crafting a narrative about those events, they will apply significantly different interpretive frames, or what some would call spin.

Every narrative or interpretation is inevitably distortive because when crafting a narrative, without quite a bit of mind-training, we simply can't help but apply spin. The spin we have on any given event, any series of events, or any given dynamic between people, is deeply influenced by the totality of our experience, especially our saṃskāras. When we tell stories, we're all spin doctors in that even when we're telling the story of our experience as honestly as we can (which itself is not so common), the way we understand that experience is profoundly influenced by everything we've ever thought, believed, and experienced up to that moment. This is why people come up with such markedly distinct narratives. In literature and film, this has become known as the Rashōmon effect. The lack of understanding of this effect produces surprise, shock, bewilderment, suspicion, and/or outrage when we hear the other person's

When we tell stories, we're all spin doctors.

version of events. But they might well be speaking in good faith and having a similar experience vis-à-vis your version of events.

The most important confounding factor in the formation of our interpretations is the self-serving ego. Our instinct for telling self-serving stories (which is another version of spin) can operate unconsciously, or it can be calculated. Both are common, but the first is probably more common—and harder to deal with—because the person really believes what they're saying. You, dear reader, are almost definitely a case study of this, just like everyone else. I'll give some examples.

The self-serving ego is almost constantly in play when describing human behavior. It manifests in what is often called emotive conjugation, first described clearly by Bertrand Russell in 1948. When describing the very same behavior or attitude, Russell argued, we use words with different valences depending on whether we're describing ourselves, our interlocutor, or someone not present (and not liked), for example:

- "I am firm, you are obstinate, and he is pigheaded."
- "I have reconsidered the matter, you have changed your mind, and he has gone back on his word."
- "I stand up for myself, you won't take no for an answer, and she always needs to get her way."
- "I am highly observant, you are detail oriented, and he is a nitpicker."

Or sometimes, if the third person is highly thought of, we see a different version of emotive conjugation, that is perhaps self-serving in a much subtler way, such as "I perspire, you sweat, and she glows."

Examples could, of course, be multiplied endlessly. Notice that tribalism also plays into this because one's social group is part of one's ego structure: a politician you support reconsidered the matter in light of new evidence, but the politician you don't support flip-flopped.

It is in precisely this sense that all our news sources have become partisan, and therefore they are all bad-faith actors. Far from compensating for the human tendency toward emotive conjugation, they are using it to pander to their audiences, and even weaponizing it.* But it's important to understand that the self-serving ego is very good at concealing itself, creating what we might call a cognitive blind spot. Because of this, we tend to be convinced that our verbal assessments are mostly fair and balanced and based in reality, at least compared to those of others, and we tend to believe that our preferred news outlets are reliable. It's vital that we learn to compensate for our individual and collective tendency toward emotive conjugation. It's a

All our news sources have become partisan, and therefore they are all bad-faith actors.

*As Eric Weinstein wrote, "[Frank Luntz found that] many if not most people form their opinions based solely on whatever [emotive] Russell conjugation is presented to them and *not* on the underlying facts. That is, the very same person will oppose a 'death tax' while having supported an 'estate tax' seconds earlier, even though these taxes are two descriptions of the exact same underlying object. Further, such is the power of emotive conjugation that we are generally not even aware that we hold such contradictory opinions. Thus 'illegal aliens' and 'undocumented immigrants' may be the same people, but the former label leads to calls for deportation while the latter one instantly causes many of us to consider amnesty programs and paths to citizenship. If we accept that Russell Conjugation keeps us from even seeing that we do not hold consistent opinions on facts, we see a possible new answer to a puzzle that dates from the birth of the [world wide] web: 'If the internet democratized information, why has its social impact been so much slower than many of us expected?' Assuming that our actions are based not on what we know but upon how we feel about what we know, we see that traditional media has all but lost control of gate-keeping our information, but not yet how it is emotively shaded. In fact, it [would be] relatively simple to write a computer program to crawl factually accurate news stories against a look-up table of Russell conjugates to see the exact bias of every supposedly objective story. Thus the answer to the puzzle of our inaction may be that we built an information superhighway for all, but neglected to build an empathy network alongside it to democratize what we feel." See edge.org/response-detail/27181. The reader will please note that while I agree with Weinstein's words on this particular topic (as quoted here), he is, as of this writing, a managing director of Thiel Capital, which this author considers deeply morally compromised to say the least, there being substantial evidence that Peter Thiel harbors views, and covertly supports causes, that promote fascism, racism, eugenics, and misogyny.

form of storytelling that exacerbates division and outrage at a time when we need unity and understanding more than ever.

Since in this analysis second-order reality constitutes interpretation of direct experience, we must of course consider interpretations based on eyewitness reports as third-order reality and thus even more potentially problematic. That is say, narratives based on other people's narratives are potentially subject to double the number of distorting factors. This is why good journalism is so extraordinarily rare, and also why gossip can be so damaging for all kinds of organizations.

True and False

Despite all I've said on the matter, we must admit that every single story ever told, every single interpretation ever offered, must be considered simultaneously false and true. False in the ways I already described (and in more ways that I haven't described), but also true in the sense that if we bothered to unpack it, every single sentence of the narrative with which we represent ourselves or others corresponds to some aspect of our lived experience (assuming we are formulating those narratives in good faith, with our best attempt at honesty). Such unpacking needs to proceed with utmost patience and care to get at any underlying truth, but there is some truth-value to nearly everything we say about our experience because every single sentence uttered in good faith can be linked to some specific moment of real experience. Psychologist Marshall Rosenberg argued, for example, that negative judgments of others are best viewed as distorted expressions of our own difficult emotions and unmet needs. To cite some simplistic examples, the truth-value to be mined from the judgment "You're a slob" directed at a housemate or family member, say, is something like "I'm angry because I want to live in a clean house, and I can't see you supporting that goal in any way." The truth-value to be mined from the judgment "You're selfish" is something like "I'm upset because I want you to pay more attention to other people's needs than I see you doing." The second-person judgment always points back to something true in first-person experience, and in that sense, every story, opinion, and judgment has some hidden truth-value. No one has ever literally been "selfish" because that is a one-word story with which we clumsily represent our own experience of dissatisfaction with that person's behavior. And when we call someone selfish to their face, it is a tactic of attempted manipulation: we're hoping to shame them into behavior that we find more palatable. This is painfully ironic, considering that we would have a much better chance of influencing them in the desired direction by simply articulating the truth of our first-person experience as honestly as we can.

I do not mean to suggest by this argument that some behaviors are not better than others by any demonstrable measure. I think it's a good idea to call behaviors that are likely contribute to the well-being of yourself and others beneficial and to call behaviors that are likely to decrease or impede the well-being of yourself and others detrimental. But these labels are effective, and we might even say true, relative to a presumed goal, that of human well-being (or the well-being of conscious creatures more generally). Therefore, labels of *beneficial* or *detrimental* (or their near enemies, *good* and *bad* or *right* and *wrong*) cannot constitute objective truths that exist irrespective of a specific context, however much we might wish otherwise. This section is concerned with the pursuit of truth, and the value of parsing first- and second-order reality in that context. But I also suggest that the ability to perform such parsing is beneficial as previously defined . When we can distinguish first- and second-order reality, we can take responsibility for our own inner experience and give feedback to others who impact that experience in ways that are more likely to be effective. Even more significantly, with this ability, we can become free of the mind-world and enjoy the astonishing mode of being that we might characterize as communion with reality as such, also known as awakeness.

Now, as you might have already realized, by the logic of this argument, it must be equally true that positive judgments of others are also distorted expressions of our own inner experience, in this case pleasurable feelings that arise from having our needs met. So if you say another person is "wonderful" or "kind," the truth-value that can be mined from that statement is that you are having pleasurable feelings that arise from the way that person meets your needs or nourishes your values. These sorts of interpersonal judgments are regarded as positive or unproblematic because they don't seem to cause harm. Except that they do cause a subtle kind of harm, as all distortions of reality inevitably do, I argue. When you eulogize someone else, you subtly (or obviously) pedestalize them, placing them at some distance from yourself. This makes it harder to recognize that your appreciation of them is based in shared values that you have with them. That recognition would probably bring about a feeling of connection, whereas pedestalization contributes to a sense of separation and therefore alienation.

To summarize, there's no such thing as a thought or a verbal statement that is totally true (apart, perhaps, from verbal statements that effectively approximate sound and valid mathematical equations or formulae). But there are interpretations that illuminate our individual or collective experience more effectively than others. We consider insights into our individual experience to have a different quality or character than insights into our collective experience. This doesn't necessarily mean we need to consider the latter truer than the former. While a valid insight into one person's lived experience might be seen as trivial, the more ground even a well-tested generalization seeks to cover, the more it must be watered down until approaches banality. I argue that we must always keep in view that thoughts or narratives are best viewed as tools rather than truths, to avoid the common conflation of first- and second-order reality. It simply is the case that some thoughts or narratives are articulated in such a way as to help people more effectively understand their experience and make peace with it. And perhaps, in the final analysis, that's really what we mean by truth, whether personal or scientific: propositions and interpretations that are more effective at helping people understand their experience. And we could define that understanding as truthful in terms of its ability to help us make peace with the past and more effectively navigate the future.

Gaslighting

We can conclude this section by considering the phenomenon that has become known as gaslighting. This term, derived from the 1944 film *Gaslight* (which is worth seeing, by the way), rightly refers to the act of undermining someone's interpretation of their experience so cleverly or thoroughly that they begin to doubt their own experience and, in extreme cases, their own sanity. In the strict usage of the term, gaslighting is a form of lying: you know the other person's interpretation is valid (as far as interpretations go, anyway), but you systematically sow seeds of self-doubt in them for reasons of your own, even implying that they might be delusional. However, these days the term is thrown around carelessly and sometimes even weaponized. For example, someone who is mounting an effective counterargument might be accused of gaslighting, especially by someone who conflates their experience and their interpretation of their experience and who, therefore, believes that their interlocutor has no right to question their interpretation at all. It might be a fine line at times, but there's an important difference between questioning somebody's interpretation of their experience out of curiosity to get at the underlying truth versus questioning their interpretation as a power play—a manipulative attempt to systematically undermine their confidence in their own contemplative process.

Gaslighting is always a manipulative act based in the presumption that your interpretation of their experience is better than theirs, and in the desire to supplant their interpretation with your own in service of your agenda, which often entails having power over them. Gaslighting is almost always a bid for power in a relationship. The frightening thing is that we can do this without even realizing that we're doing it. It takes honest self-reflection combined with openness to the possibility of being wrong to uncover this phenomenon in oneself. Before engaging in this self-reflection, I gaslighted people frequently, and even after this self-reflection, I can't claim to have become totally free of this insidious habit. I am sure that many others who have honestly self-reflected on this issue would say the same. And it does seem to be the case that any form of unearned privilege (based on ethnicity, gender, etc.) exacerbates the likelihood that one commits this sin against the truth, often without realizing one is doing so.

I would suggest that we humans instinctively engage in power plays of various kinds until we train ourselves not to—or until we reach a point in the awakening process where we have lost the ability to believe in hierarchies and likewise have lost the desire to wield power over others because of seeing with clarity that that particular belief is purely a mental construct and that that particular desire does not contribute to well-being.

Let's explore the fine line here more carefully. To begin with, we must allow that it is possible to question someone's interpretation of their experience (or have them question yours) without it being a manipulative bid for more power in the relationship, however rare that might in fact be. Investigating this requires us to look into the difficult and subtle question of our underlying motivation. We must ask ourselves, "Am I coming from an honest desire to know the truth, out of care for both myself and the other person? Am I curious to see what happens when we dig under these mind-formed interpretations to undercover the visceral lived experience? Or am I seeking to advance my interpretation at the expense of theirs because I love to be 'right' or because I want the upper hand?"

Even if your motive is pure, when you question someone's interpretation of their experience, they might become upset, especially when they feel a strong emotional charge in the relationship of their story to their lived experience. When their story is emotionally charged in this way, being, for example, an interpretation of the reasons for very painful experiences that is sanctioned by their social group, then if you question their interpretation, they can only regard it as gaslighting. It feels as if you're doubting their experience itself, even if you're not. You're treading on very delicate ground.

How to make this conversational ground firmer? I would say that questioning somebody's interpretation of their experience is valid only when they give consent for you to do just that and when you've checked your motive for doing so. Both are necessary, and neither is sufficient on its own. If people tell their story and you question it without their consent, it's not going to go well, even if that story deserves to be questioned in general.

Interpretations of reality deserve to be questioned when they are unsupported by evidence (or supported by insufficient evidence to warrant the conclusions being drawn) and are likely to cause harm of one kind or another. Here, too, both conditions are necessary, and neither is sufficient on its own. One might argue, why not question interpretations that are harmless but likely to be wrong (that is, unsupported by sufficient evidence)? Because that's a waste of time and energy when we face global problems and existential risks that require more and more unity on our part to negotiate successfully.

One of the most useful and meaningful definitions of awakeness is this ability to distinguish between first- and second-order reality. If that distinction is authentically available to you but it's not yet available to your interlocutor, then that can be frustrating. The other person might perceive you as positioning yourself as having superior knowledge or wisdom because you're trying to talk about discerning something that doesn't make sense to them. You're seeing a bright line that they don't see. If they're not persuaded that that line exists, and that you have some ability to see it, they might even suspect you of playing mind games with them for nefarious (or deluded) reasons of your own. I do not think such conversations can prove fruitful. There's no point in trying to point out a distinction that others don't believe in and don't yet want to see.

These are challenging issues to negotiate because even though first-order reality is always simple (indeed, it's that which cannot be simpler), second-order reality is always complicated. Teasing out the precise relationships between our mental structures of representation with that which they seek to represent is one of the most difficult things we can do. It calls on our intellectual capacities, it calls on our intuitive capacities, and it calls on our capacity for clear self-reflection, which is often not nearly as available to us as we'd like to think it is.

Even though it's still rare among humans, the easy part here is seeing the difference between what presents in direct experience and our representation (i.e., interpretation) of it. The hard part is clearly seeing the nature of the relationship between these two—the surprisingly tenuous threads that connect various aspects of the interpretation to experience itself in highly complex and nuanced and culturally contingent ways. These threads connect the interpretation to not only the reality the interpretation purports to represent but also everything else in the person who is making the representation.

There is no perfect way to communicate direct experience because of the nature of language itself. We can't even adequately describe a simple sensual experience, like the taste of a mango, to someone who has never had it, let alone the nuances of our experience of love or of the subtleties of human connection. When we've grokked this, we stop searching for stable truths (or universal truth) in the thought-world, and we evaluate articulable thoughts solely in terms of their efficacy.

When you clearly see the real but nonconceptual difference between experience and interpretation, it radically impacts your life. It radically transfigures the way you experience reality. If you see the difference between first- and second-order reality, then you realize that nothing is what you think it is. "A tree is not my concept of it." Then you ask yourself, "What actually is it?" And then you realize that you don't know because the only answers that arise are more words, which are concepts, and that's not what a tree is or what it's made of. Then lightning strikes: "I don't know what anything is!" What is anything apart from your concept of it? When you genuinely tap into this inquiry-cum-realization, you launch into a world of profoundly wondrous unknowing. If you're ready for it, it's a state of exquisite aliveness. That state doesn't render all your interpretations wholly meaningless because, again, there might be value in teasing out why you interpret things the way you do. But reality itself is just . . . pure is-ness. Words fail. There aren't even objects anymore, since you see that objects are concepts. As a result, you see that everything is ultimate reality and nothing is separable. If the word *God* makes sense to you, you see everything as the direct and immediate manifestation of God. Or the Absolute. The words don't matter. You see that the One manifests as everything we experience before we have a thought about it—and then it manifests as all our thoughts about it.

Enlightenment

FOREMOST AMONG THE SINGLE-WORD NEAR ENEMIES, for meditators and those on spiritual paths derived from Asian traditions, is the word *enlightenment*. Misunderstanding the meaning and usage of this word can constitute a real hindrance on the spiritual path, and understanding why it's the wrong word (and why *awakening* is a better one) entails insights into the purpose of spiritual practice that constitute considerable assets on the journey.

The definition of the word *enlightenment*, in its spiritual sense (as opposed to its rationalist sense), is given in the *Oxford English Dictionary* (and several others) as: "the action or state of attaining or having attained spiritual knowledge or insight." Under this definition, the word is definitely a near enemy of the truth. First, given the assumption that knowledge is something expressed in words or other symbols, there is no knowledge that could be imparted that would bring about enlightenment. If there were, that knowledge would have been discovered by now and most of humanity would be enlightened, just like most of humanity can do basic arithmetic. Second, and more importantly, the existence of the noun *enlightenment* implies a definitive end, a final state in which one has reached the ultimate insight and knows the secret of existence, and it further implies a binary opposition with a state of "unenlightenment." In this misconstrued paradigm, there are only two states: you're either enlightened or you're not. If that's what you believe to be the case, then you are likely to strive mightily to attain this imagined ultimacy, which is a problem because both the action of striving and the concept of an attainment undermine the possibility of spiritual awakening. Furthermore, you're also likely to believe that this putative attainment would elevate you above the mass of humans or exalt you somehow, and this kind of hierarchical thinking is also antithetical to spiritual awakening.

But there's an even more insidious effect of this misunderstanding. Most of those who assume this definition of enlightenment imagine that it doesn't represent anything that is possible for them in this lifetime. In other words, the putative state of enlightenment has become so overglorified and mythologized that most practitioners of yoga, meditation, and mindfulness today don't consider it as a serious possibility for themselves, and the ones who do tend to have heavily inflated egos. And those ancient and modern figures commonly held out as examples of "complete enlightenment," like the Buddha and Ramana Maharshi, are so severely pedestalized that people don't see in them a mirror of what's possible for any human being sufficiently interested.

I would propose that enlightenment is a near enemy of the truth that I (and some others) like to call abiding awakeness. But this is not about using the "right" language. It's about understanding what we mean by these words, and specifically why the connotations of one term might be more beneficial than that of another. Here I want to argue that spiritual awakening constitutes a spectrum with an indefinite number of points along it, and consequently, awakening is possible for anyone and more awakeness is possible for anyone already awake.

The first order of business, then, is to define exactly what we mean by the word *awakening* (and its related forms, like *awakeness*). The word *awakening* has now become so common in some circles that it's easy to forget that it is in fact a metaphor for something for which we literally don't have any native word in English (or any European language). It's a metaphor that implies that whatever we're talking about is analogous to waking up from a dream. The analogy is a good one for reasons I'll describe later, but let's remember that no analogy is ever perfect.

At this point, you may be wondering about the Sanskrit word that scholars of the nineteenth and twentieth centuries translated as "enlightenment." That word is *bodha* (or its synonym *bodhi*), which in fact means "being awake." The choice to translate it as "enlightenment" in the nineteenth century was influenced by the European usage of the word in reference to the philosophical movement of the eighteenth century known as the Enlightenment, even though the latter had little in common with the Buddhist and Hindu philosophies that use the word *bodha*. For those who wish to know the full semantic range of the Sanskrit term, *bodha* is glossed in dictionaries as the following: waking, becoming or being awake, the waking state, consciousness, the opening of a blossom, wisdom, perception, apprehension, thought, knowledge, understanding, intelligence, instruction, or advice, depending on the context. So, in the original language, there's no bright line between the concept of awakening and that of awareness per se. The meaning of the word *bodha* depended on context, as did its cognate *buddha*, which simply meant "awakened" in not only the spiritual sense but also (and more often) the everyday physical sense of having woken up from a night's sleep.

Spiritual awakening constitutes a spectrum with an indefinite number of points along it.

Having established, I hope, that the translation "awake" or "awakening" is most appropriate for *bodha*, what the heck is it? I will define it below in five ways, but first I have to say this: if you haven't yet entered the awakening process, you may be tempted to regard it as a myth, a carrot dangled by a guru who wants your money, a psychological delusion, an imaginary concept leveraged by self-important spiritual types to self-aggrandize and engage in power dynamics, or perhaps a temporary experience like an altered state of consciousness. But to you I say that awakening is real, and it has nothing to do with any of those things (though all those things do happen as well). It is not a psychological state or a peak experience. In fact, strange as it may sound, it's not an experience at all. Awakeness is a specific mode of experiencing—a different paradigm of being, we could say.

Now the language I've just used seems to contradict what I said before, that awakening is a spectrum not a binary. But now it's time to clarify that it's both. It's a binary in the sense that the awakening process has either begun or it hasn't, and it's a spectrum in the sense that once it has begun, it constitutes a continuum with an indefinite number of points. It's also important to note that this continuum has several tipping points that we might call phases of awakening, as long as we understand that they don't happen in the same order for everyone who undergoes them (and, of course, not everyone who awakens undergoes all of them). It's also important to note that many people who believe they are awake have not yet even begun the awakening process. This misunderstanding occurs when people confuse understanding and believing in spiritual philosophy with awakeness, which is very common. This phenomenon is discussed in "Reality" (see page 185).

So, what is awakening if it's not an experience or a specific kind of knowledge? We could say that it is a paradigm shift that reconfigures the way you experience everything. It gets confused with a type of experience because there are often significant, even dramatic, experiential elements that accompany this paradigm shift. But these experiential elements are impermanent whereas awakeness itself can become one's permanent place of residence, as it were. How is this possible? Didn't the Buddha teach that everything is impermanent?

No, he taught that nirvāṇa is permanent, precisely because it's not the presence of something; it's the absence of something, namely delusion and confusion about the nature of reality and/or the nature of selfhood. Everything that comes into being passes away, of course, but something that can cease to be can be gone forever. That's why *nirvāṇa* literally means "cessation." Delusion has ceased, and its cessation constitutes a different paradigm of being. But of course, for most people it doesn't cease all at once (despite the mythic stories of "sudden enlightenment"). There can be a sudden rupture in the nature of experience that initiates the awakening process, but delusion is worn away slowly through a process of attrition driven by (the right kind of) spiritual practice.

Awakening accompanied by experiential fireworks and awakening accompanied by a lack thereof are the same in terms of where they land you. But where is that? While the discourse around the word *enlightenment* (and the discourse of the spiritual marketplace) makes it seem as though the enlightened person knows something—or has something—the unenlightened person doesn't, it's the other way around. Awakening entails *losing* something—specifically, your deeply conditioned beliefs about who you are and what the world is—and gaining nothing but the clarity of vision that naturally results from that loss. In this sense, it can be compared to the surgery that removes a cataract from the eye.

Of course, what I've just said is an oversimplification, but it's impossible to talk about this without oversimplifying. Whatever metaphor we use is in some way inadequate.

Now I'll talk about five different versions of awakening, which can be seen as phases of the same process. Remember, our primary governing metaphor here, used by countless spiritual teachers, is that of waking up from a dream. Why is that the central metaphor? In a normal dream, you don't know that you're dreaming, and so you don't know that everything that's happening is generated by your own mind. You don't know that everyone in the dream is an aspect of your own psyche, and so you may feel fear when menaced by a villain or a monstrous creature and you may desire a sexy person. But when you wake up from a literal dream, you realize its nature. You might contemplate the dream and even sift through it for potential insights, but you are no longer afraid or aroused (though in the case of intense dreams, it can take some time for your nervous system to settle down upon awakening—which is also a salient part of this analogy).

In some sense you judge the dream as not being real, at least not in comparison to your current experience. In the same way, then, spiritual awakening shifts your relationship to the whole of reality. It doesn't seem real in the way it did before, and it can no longer affect you in the way that it did. There's also often an enormous sense of relief, as when waking up from a bad dream. But in some ways, spiritual awakening is not as analogous to physical awakening as it is to the transition into lucid dreaming. You're still in the dream, but you know it's a dream, so you know that everything is a manifestation of your consciousness and there's nothing to be afraid of, so you can basically do what you like and just enjoy the ride. But it's also not like that because, if you take that metaphor too literally, then awakening is just the transition into solipsism, and that's not what we're talking about, either. Whichever way we use the metaphor, it dead-ends at some point, and we have to admit that even the best metaphor can't entirely capture what we're talking about. So, let's look at a different way to describe awakening.

The purpose of trying to describe these versions or phases of awakening, despite the fact that it's impossible to do so perfectly, is twofold: one, so that people who've undergone them will recognize that what they've undergone is in fact part of a universal process that is simply an intrinsic potentiality within human consciousness, and two, so that those who haven't yet undergone them will be equipped with signposts so that, down the road, they will know that they're not actually going crazy. This *is* a universal process: though the details can vary, and elements of it are certainly mediated by the culturally specific context in which awakening occurs, it's a process that is possible for anyone in any culture to undergo. Some people need to hear about its possibility before the awakening process can begin, while others can start experiencing it out of the blue.

The fact that this process can initiate itself spontaneously in just about anyone, including someone without prior exposure to the kinds of ideas found in this book, constitutes a profound mystery. I hope this mystery will become a central object of study for neuroscience since the awakening process, for many people, also has physiological symptoms or side effects that indicate it is just as much a neurobiological process as a spiritual or psychological one.

Lastly, by presenting these versions or phases of awakening, I'm not claiming to offer a definitive map, just a clear and useful one that covers much of the terrain in simple language.

> **First version/phase: Waking up out of the socially constructed self.** This means waking up out of the belief that your thoughts, memories, self-images, or narratives about your life define you, delimit you, or even describe you in your real nature. This means waking up out of the dream that the contents of thought have anything to do with what you fundamentally are. This entails seeing clearly that all the "I" thoughts—all the thoughts about what you are, what sort of person you are, how good or bad you are—are nothing but thoughts, none of which touch the deep beingness that you are. In this phase, one clearly sees that the concept of "me" doesn't point to anything but an ill-defined, fabricated, nebulous, and contradictory idea of self—that is to say, a thought. A thought that somehow sits on top of and veils your deeper being. Like all the versions or phases of awakening, this realization is, in truth, nonconceptual, but it necessarily sounds conceptual

when expressed in words.* Upon seeing that 'me' is a mental construct, one may react with sudden fear and resistance, or one may suddenly experience a state of pure being, which we could also call awareness-presence. Some traditions call this state of pure being free of self-image or self-consciousness 'true self,' others call it 'no self.' For one who's had this awakening, it doesn't matter what we call it.

Second version/phase: Waking up out of unconscious conceptual overlay. This means no longer projecting your concepts of things onto things without realizing that you're doing so. For example, seeing the difference between the concept "tree" and the always unique and inexpressible realities pointed to (but not encompassed) by that word. By the same token, in this phase, one no longer reduces people to the concepts one has about them or conflates them with one's stories about them. This is simply the natural extension of the first stage. We could characterize it as the realization that just as you are not your story about yourself, no one else is your story about them, and the world is not your story about it. Nothing is your concept of it. Concepts might be useful pragmatically speaking, but nothing, not even the simplest thing, like a table or a tree, is reducible to your concept of it.** Eventually one realizes the implications of this: thoughts are tools, not truths. Even after

---

*A nonconceptual realization is one that takes place, one might say, in a *subitist* manner, in the same way that one sees that the grass is green without having to think 'green,' or that there are three objects before you without having to count them. This realization can happen spontaneously, or someone might point out to you that 'me' is just a thought, and if you're ripe for realization, you look within and simply see that it's true.

**Not that a table or a tree is simple in actuality; in fact, that's the whole point here. The mind reduces a complex phenomenon like a tree, which is inseparably wedded to its total environment and embedded in a vast network of causes and conditions, to a simple conceptual object: tree. But in truth there is no such object. The mental representation of the world is like a simplistic map, and *map is not territory*.

having had this realization, thoroughly freeing oneself from the habit of unconscious conceptual overlay takes a long time.

Third version/phase: Waking up out of the dream of separation. Having realized that everything is part of a process that always escapes your conceptualization of it (there are in truth only verbs, not nouns, one might say) and that all categories and demarcations are mental constructs, one then sees that separation is itself nothing but a thought. Without the belief in separation, it's impossible to experience loneliness or any kind of existential alienation. By shedding the belief that anything could be separate from you, you awaken to the always-already-existent truth of seamless unity with all that is. Though this particular version or phase of awakening is often glorified in the literature (usually under the rubric of unity-consciousness) because it tends to produce quite a lot of bliss and joy as a by-product. In actuality it's just our natural state of being: seeing clearly without the filter of the culturally and linguistically conditioned mind. To be technically accurate, you don't attain unity; you experientially recognize that you have never been separate from anything ever. Fully absorbing the implications of that is permanently paradigm shifting.

Fourth version/phase: Waking up out of the belief in (and sense of) "objective reality." In this phase or version of awakening, the world ceases to be a world—that is, the existence of an objective (observer-independent) universe made of material stuff is seen to be an illusion and it completely dissolves, leaving one with the experience that all phenomena are nothing but forms of consciousness, or appearances within the dream of the one mind. This consciousness-that-is-all does not belong to anyone, but at the same time, what you are is nothing but it. Needless to say, these words are wholly inadequate—this mode of experience is almost impossible to describe and certainly even weirder than it sounds.

Fifth version/phase: Waking up to the absolute ground of being. In this phase or version of awakening, one directly senses that all phenomena are somehow held within, and permeated by, an infinitude of still silent spacious no-thing-ness. It is the ground of being in the sense that all phenomena are made possible by it and "supported" by it, even though it is absolute no-thing-ness. (This is not possible to understand conceptually, of course.) Some people sense the ground of being as still silent *presence*—but an absolutely impersonal presence that is, at the same time, always closer than your own breath. All phenomena taken together are perceived to be something like a tiny ripple on the surface of this ocean of infinite stillness. In this mode of experiencing, which utterly transcends space and time, one also has the felt-sense that everything that ever dies or dissolves does not in fact disappear but rather merges back into the ground of being, from which it can emerge once again in the vast cycles of infinite time. This might sound like a belief when the felt-sense I'm talking about is clothed in words, but it's nothing like a belief. It's undeniable immediacy, more immediate than even the phrase "direct experience" can convey and realer than the real.

To reiterate, these five versions of awakening can happen to people in a different order than described here, and someone might only have one of these awakenings and not the others. And there are other ways of mapping this terrain as well. One traditional map presents what I've talked about here in just three phases, while others teach as many as ten stages (including stages of integrating the above realizations into everyday life), and still others declare that thinking of the awakening process in terms of stages is invalid. I think maps are valuable as long as you remember that map is not territory. You can't drink the word *water*, you can't live in the blueprint of a house, and likewise, understanding and believing spiritual teachings is nothing like experiencing the states that gave rise to those teachings in the first place. Though that distinction might seem obvious to you, the confusion of map with territory is commonplace: it is exactly such confusion that causes people to take the words of scripture and holy books literally, giving rise to dogmatism and religious fundamentalism. And most humans today are liable to such literalism.

I've tried to make clear here that these versions or stages of awakening don't have the experiential quality of a download of knowledge or an attainment of any kind. They have the experiential quality of more and more illusion being stripped away, leaving reality utterly laid bare, stark, and yet somehow much more vivid. Ineffably shining. Some call this "naked awareness," others "primordial purity."

Awakeness, then, is not another interpretation of reality that one acquires and then finds a way to integrate with one's existing knowledge. Taking all the phases together and considering them as part of a single process, we can say awakening is a paradigm shift that utterly obliterates all your stories about reality and launches you into an indescribable mode of being in which the only true knowing is predicated upon unknowing everything you ever thought you knew. This nonconceptual knowing is a kind of spontaneous immediacy in which the distinction between knowing and being collapses, resulting in raw and vivid intimacy with absolutely everything, free of the need to understand or interpret it, and free of the need to accept or reject it.

Awakening is a paradigm shift that utterly obliterates all your stories about reality.

When people hear such a description, though, they imagine that this must constitute a kind of transcendental mindless state that couldn't possibly be compatible with functioning in the world. But this is entirely untrue and is a supposition based in a lack of direct experience of the paradigm shift alluded to here. "Free of the need to understand and interpret" and other such phrases doesn't mean you don't have thoughts in this state, and it doesn't mean you can't utilize concepts as skillfully as anyone else. It just means that those thoughts and concepts are not determinative of your experience of reality. You are free of the compulsion to seek truth in mental representations of reality.

In the awakened mode, thoughts no longer constitute truths, but the best of them do constitute tools, and some of them are more effective than others. In ancient times, myths were stories that communicated the values of a society. They were tools to communicate those values. In spiritual texts, thoughts are tools used to point toward ways of experiencing the world that one might not have realized are possible. In your own life, thoughts can be tools that facilitate human connection and intuitive understanding—but they cannot do so if they are taken too literally, that is, if we fail to see that they are tools, not truths. In this view, then, a thought that is more effective than another in a particular context can be considered truer (in that context), even though it isn't ever literally true. When there is understanding of this, a person can exist in a radically different paradigm and still function effectively in our complex society—that is, after transitioning through an adjustment period in which certain types of functioning (especially social interactions) can be temporarily impaired.

Having said this, it's also the case that one who is awake to any significant degree will find that it's now impossible to continue doing anything that feels untrue or out of alignment, for lack of a better phrase. You can no longer effectively lie to yourself in this state. So, some who enter the awakening process discover that they have been terribly unhappy with their marriage or their career but managed to convince themselves that that's just life, and you've got to grin and bear it—and they no longer can. This is why, in some cases, a person's life might seem to fall apart in the early stages of awakening, and their friends and family are understandably concerned. But for some people, that is a necessary part of the process. This should not, of course, be taken to mean that someone's life falling apart is itself evidence of awakening.

There's something about this paradigm shift called awakening that compels you toward truth, sometimes almost against your will. You realize that there is such a thing as truth, though it's not doctrinal or ideological, and there's a sense of being compelled to discern its nature as best as one can, in all possible dimensions, whether or not what is discerned is ultimately even articulatable.

I'll conclude by resolving an apparent contradiction in this teaching. Awakening is, by its very nature, both sudden and gradual. It's sudden in the sense that nonconceptual truth of any kind is necessarily seen all at once, in a single moment, but the process of integrating what one has realized into one's psyche and one's life is necessarily gradual. Integration is the gradual process of seeing everything anew in the light of one's awakened awareness and allowing one's understanding of any and every aspect of life to recalibrate itself in that light, in that new context. For example, when re-examining a relationship dynamic in this new context, what was previously muddy and confusing becomes simple and clear, and even if that clarity is not articulatable, it nonetheless enables a shift in the dynamic of relating.

Insights and realizations are the enjoyable part of this process. Integration is, for many, the hard part. But it is the process of integrating these profound insights into the nature of reality that is most thoroughly life-changing. Without integration, even powerful insights can just . . . fade away. And without a teacher and community to support integration, one's nonconceptual realizations can be co-opted by the mind and turned into mere beliefs that may bolster an inflated self-image or "spiritual ego."

Most importantly (for those who care about the well-being of others, anyway), without integration, your awakening is unlikely to substantially benefit anyone else. It's almost as if, despite having discovered the most exquisite fountain of beatific light within yourself, it can't effectively flow out to uplift and benefit others until the psyche is brought into greater alignment with that light, just as water cannot effectively flow to a new destination if the channels along which it flows are not aligned. This is just a metaphor, of course. But it does seem that everything needs to be recalibrated in light of what you've realized at each major stage of awakening. This recalibration can be very subtle in some respects and obvious in others, depending on the person. How does it happen? By looking at everything in your life (and in your own psyche) afresh, from the perspective of what's been realized. If you're truly willing to do that—and sometimes it isn't easy because you'll inevitably end up grieving the unconscious behaviors through which you have caused others pain—then transformation inevitably follows.

Ego

MISUNDERSTANDINGS ABOUT THE concept of ego are rife in spiritual communities today. Now, when I say misunderstandings, I specifically mean relative to the teachings on ego in the Yoga traditions. There's no possibility of misunderstandings of this issue in any absolute sense because "ego" is not an objective category. It's a culturally constructed category, and it is constructed in different ways by different cultures and for different purposes.

Let's clarify what this term means in Yoga philosophy particularly and then talk about why it's important. Please lay aside anything that you've heard about the ego from Western psychology from Freudian or Jungian teachings. It's not to say that those teachings don't have value for some people, but you need to lay them aside to really grasp what is meant by the term *ego* in the Yogic sense of the word. Here we're talking about terminology originally articulated in the Sanskrit language. The term corresponding to *ego* in Sanskrit is *ahaṃkāra,* which is itself a specialized compound of two words: *aham,* which means "I," and *kāra,* which means "maker" or "manufacturer." So *ahaṃkāra* means "self-image manufacturer" or, even more literally,

"I-maker." Primary sources in Yoga philosophy explicate the ego as an aspect of mind, specifically as that part of the mind that generates self-images ("I am this kind of person, not that kind") and self-referential thoughts ("Did I just come off like an idiot?" or "What does this say about me?" or "That reminds me of the time I . . .").

Believing these thoughts and giving credence to one's self-images gives rise to the feeling of being a separate self. Usually, self-referential thoughts are compulsively believed. If you're well into the process of awakening, sometimes you believe them and sometimes you don't, and there can come a point in that process where you no longer believe any self-image-based thoughts. You stop seeing those thoughts (whether positive or negative) as describing a truth about your putative "self." but you can still discern whether any of them might be a useful tool. For example, you might notice a judgmental thought about yourself and immediately identify it as a thought and therefore not a truth, but you can still engage in an inquiry that proves useful, such as "Ah, that thought is based on what so-and-so said about me—does their judgment, however distorted, point out a behavior that upon consideration I feel called to change?"—while being free of any sense of shame or wrongness.

The important thing here is that from the Yogic point of view, the ego is nothing but a persistent conglomeration of thoughts about one's "self" that are believed. But the self to which those thoughts refer is itself a mental construct based primarily on social interactions (or, more precisely, the internalization of what others have said about us). In assessing the degree of egotism one possesses, we could say that if 40 percent of a person's thoughts are self-referential, they are more egotistical than someone whose thoughts are 30 percent self-referential, assuming both individuals are mind-identified, as most people are. From the perspective of Yoga philosophy, the question of whether the self-referential thoughts are self-denigrating or self-aggrandizing is irrelevant. Some who has many self-denigrating thoughts (and believes them) is just as egotistical as someone who has many self-aggrandizing thoughts—and both kinds of thoughts cause suffering more or less equally (a fact that becomes more apparent if we put the suffering of others on equal footing with one's own suffering). Many of the self-referential thoughts that calcify into self-images are linked to saṃskāras, those impressions in the psyche of unresolved or undigested past experiences that influence which self-referential thoughts we find compelling.

These days, some folks are saying that the ego is necessary because it is the means by which one interfaces with society and with other humans. They see this assertion as a beneficial pushback against the Yogic claim that the ego should be dissolved. Some even claim that we couldn't function without the ego. But what's really going on here is a confusion of definition. Such people are implicitly defining the ego in a way that draws more from Western (specifically Freudian) psychological discourse. But there is only a partial overlap with the way these terms are defined in Western psychology and in the Yoga traditions. The ego, from the Yogic point of view, is like an obscuring cloud of largely unwarranted self-concern that interposes itself between you and others and oftentimes impedes the deep connection with them that we crave. This perspective on the ego is basically the opposite of "that which allows us to interface with other humans."

Self-Images

Let's define *ego* even more precisely. Since it's a function of the mind, ego is not an entity but something the mind does (and can stop doing). It's a verb, not a noun. It's the functional capacity, on the part of the mind, to generate and maintain self-images. If those self-images are believed, they can become persistent. Even then, the ego is not actually a thing; it's not a static entity. Rather, it is a collection of self-images that are persistently refreshed, maintained, justified, rationalized, and defended. It takes considerable mental-emotional energy, considerable life-energy, to maintain one's self-images, so they constitute a significant energy drain. The freer you are of self-images, the less your life-energy gets devoured by ego maintenance.

If we were to define the ego as a noun, as a figure of speech or a convenient way of talking, then it would be comparable to a raft of self-images bound together with the rope and glue of our saṃskāras—unresolved past experiences. So, what are self-images, really? They are, simply, any recurrent thought that you have about yourself, whether simple or complex. These thoughts are related to a whole raft of culturally conditioned assumptions that are so deeply internalized we are scarcely conscious of them. Anything that you would put after the words "I am" constitutes a self-image, for example: "I am a man, I am a woman, I am nonbinary, I am a yoga teacher, I am a scholar, I'm a good person, I'm a failure" and on and on. Anything that you might put after the words "I am"—regardless of whether you ever speak it aloud—is a self-image, a concept of yourself. Every self-image constitutes a self-limitation and something you feel you need to defend and justify to others. You expend precious life-force trying to convince others that your thoughts about yourself are true when they can't be. Self-referential thoughts might occasionally relate to objectively measurable traits, but that doesn't make them true (as discussed in "Reality," see page 185). Since they are inevitably laden with all sorts of culturally contingent assumptions and various kinds of self-judgment, these are not the sort of thoughts that can ever be true.

And that is what makes all self-images a source of suffering: every self-concept is freighted with the baggage of cultural conditioning relating to that particular identity, and people inevitably compare themselves to their society's ideal version of that identity and can never measure up to it. I'm not just talking about the obvious examples in the arena of vocation or profession. Even the most basic, seemingly obviously true self-concepts—like "I'm a man" or "I'm a woman"—are mental constructs of imagined selfhood informed by cultural conditioning. When we use those gender terms in social discourse, we're not referring to the biological fact of whether our reproductive systems produce sperm or ova; we're unconsciously invoking a whole raft of culturally conditioned ideas about what it means to be a man, or a woman—or anything else that can be added after "I am." Likewise, when we say "I am a mother" or "I'm married," there are whole rafts of unexamined concepts that are buried under the words. These concepts come from our cultural conditioning about what it means to be a mother, spouse, or whatever else, and they're never neutral—they include tacit assumptions about what a "good [fill in the blank]" is supposed to look like and what a "bad [fill in the blank]" looks like. These assumptions are often articulable in terms of a "should." For example, a marriage *should* be for life, so any marriage that doesn't end in someone's death is called a "failed marriage." But all should statements are cultural constructs. They are never part of first-order reality, so they are never objectively or necessarily true. And yet we suffer enormously when we don't conform to the should statements that we have internalized, especially those internalized at a young age.

All should statements are cultural constructs.

It's possible to become free of these self-images and the should statements associated with them. It's not easy, but it's possible. If you're not weighed down with culturally constructed ideas of what kind of person you're supposed to be, or how you're supposed to exemplify the roles you have chosen for yourself, it's an enormous relief. You no longer beat yourself up for failing to live up to these fabricated notions. You're free to define exactly how you want to inhabit each of your roles. Furthermore, you can be more sensitive to what is called for in reality, moment to moment, instead of attempting to conform to your mental construct of what this role (whatever it is) is supposed to look like. Instead of wasting time and energy in self-critical rumination, you are free to engage in real-life forms of interrelating that inform and deepen your sense of that role and how you want to inhabit it. Imagine if your default mode was not self-conscious self-referencing but instead relational referencing, in which you're constantly connecting to reality as it is presenting itself, moment to moment, and organically responding to what your intuition calls for in that moment, instead of going into your mind-world and asking whether you're measuring up to the mental images of the role that you've internalized from authority figures and cultural narratives.

Now, this is not to say that cultural conditioning is always wrong, or inherently bad, because it's not. But if it's not recognized as a construct to which you pressure yourself to conform, it can inhibit your access to your intuitive faculty and your natural state of freedom and contentment.

While most people agree that dissolving negative self-images is desirable (since they are so obviously debilitating), they worry that if they drop their positive self-images, such as that of being a "good person" and all the shoulds associated with that notion, then there would be no injunction to moral action. They are worried that without shoulds, they might become a horrible person who just does whatever they want, regardless of the impact on others. To my mind, this objection betrays an underlying deep cynicism (foisted on humanity by Western religion): the implicit belief that, given half a chance, humans are inherently awful. We all know that when people are carrying a lot of unresolved pain inside themselves, they can be perfectly horrible to each other, but that suggests nothing about their inherent nature. Indeed, when not overwhelmed by their own suffering, most humans are instinctively drawn to acts of love and care, however small. An idea of what a "good person" is supposed to be like is neither necessary nor sufficient to facilitate these acts. They can and do flow forth spontaneously. If you can sense that your fundamental being is in truth divine (that word being a mere approximation for something utterly ineffable, of course), then this is not going to be an objection that concerns you because you know that without a self-image, what naturally arises (given half a chance) is love, care, and the desire to connect with and support others and receive their love and care in return.

Becoming Free of Ego

When combined with honest reflection on the beneficially humbling lessons life offers us, spiritual practice really can wear away the ego structure. Becoming increasingly free of ego means becoming increasingly free of self-images—both the negative ones that disempower us and the so-called positive ones that we can't ever quite live up to. It's possible to reach a point where there are either no self-images left or the ones that remain are so thoroughly enervated that one simply can't be bothered to waste any energy on defending them. They become nothing more than inert thoughts floating on the ocean of consciousness like so much driftwood. With nothing left that needs justifying or defending, there's simply the beautiful aliveness of pure being. Someone in this state can just flow into any given situation and respond organically to what's happening without the need for a self-image of what kind of person they are or should be.

Now let's return to the concept some people argue for, that the ego is an interface by which we relate to the world and if we were to eliminate the ego we could no longer function in society. From a Yogic point of view, this idea makes no sense because anything that's natural to you doesn't require a self-image to prop it up. Any action, behavior, or pattern of behavior that is natural to you continues to exist just fine without an ego. For example, for an artist who is passionate about artistic expression, the idea of herself as an artist is more of an impediment than anything else. Likewise, a yoga teacher self-conscious about her role as "teacher" is always less effective than one who lets her skills and training express intuitively in response to the needs of the people in the class that day. Similarly, a woman can care for her children effectively without a culturally inculcated image of what a "good mother" is supposed to look like. Indeed, such concepts, which vary widely across different cultures and time periods, can even cause real harm when they encourage mothers to ignore their intuitions (as mid-twentieth century ideas based on spurious hypotheses in behavioral psychology often tended to do).

As far as I can tell, there is not a single human activity that we are better at by virtue of having a self-image. When engaged in an activity that requires skill and training, a self-image doesn't help. One's training can deploy automatically, resulting in what we have come to call a flow state, in which we forget ourselves and become absorbed in the activity. In the flow state, we are most likely to perform at the peak of our abilities.

When learning a new skill, a self-image doesn't help, either. It causes you to compare yourself to others or to the imagined future version of yourself, rather than focus on internalizing the skill itself in the manner most efficient for your body-mind.

Self-images always cause suffering.

The most innocent-seeming type of self-image is that which aligns with our real talents, abilities, and character traits. Why should we seek to shed these more or less accurate self-images? For the same reason that there's no need to wear a mask of your own face. We have, I argue, two different kinds of masks: the masks that distort or conceal truths about our character and those that depict some aspect of our real nature, yet still constitute something to hide behind and something we feel we need to defend. For example, someone who has the self-image "I'm kind and caring" and who *is* kind and caring most of the time doesn't need the self-image, which only causes needless suffering. How? No one is kind and caring all the time, and if someone criticizes one of the few unkind actions of this hypothetical individual, they will feel compelled to defend their self-image, pointing out all the times they have been kind instead of accepting the validity of the criticism in relation to the specific action in question. Self-images always cause suffering. In that regard, it doesn't matter whether they correspond with reality. You might think you need these self-images, but you can prove to yourself that you don't because, if you drop them, what's revealed is the innate spontaneity of your essence-nature expressing itself perfectly in each moment.

Approval Seeking

Many people engage in activities and actions that are not natural to them: activities that reflect the internalization of someone else's story about how they should be or activities that are an attempt to earn others' approval. Strangely, we sometimes labor in this unnatural way even when the people we're trying to please are dead and gone. Somehow, we're still trying to live up to their story about who we should be. When you see and understand that you have internalized stories about who you should be that are simply not natural to you, the corresponding self-images can fall away. This is a huge relief, since those self-images are a source of self-hatred and self-castigation.

But most of you reading this probably spend much of your time (including your vocation) doing what is natural to you. Yet it doesn't make you as happy as one might expect. This is because your self-images, your thoughts about what kind of person you are and what you do, often entail a sense of obligation. Any sense of obligation decreases intrinsic motivation. This is worth noticing. Even when you're doing something that's natural to you, if you also think that you should do it or that you have to do it, the natural joy of that activity tends to drain away. I think of this when watching Olympic athletes—most of them got involved in their sport in the first place because they enjoyed it, and none of that joy is evident on their faces when they compete. We should see in their faces a warning—or a mirror to our own life. When the activity that one once loved has become a means to living up to one's self-image, it becomes increasingly joyless. At this point in the argument, some object: "It's not about my professional self-image—I work at a job I don't love because I need to provide for my family." To which I reply, it's still all about your self-image. You believe "This is what I need to do to be a good provider, a good parent." Did you ever consider the possibility that your happiness, or lack thereof, has a bigger impact on your children than what you can or can't buy them?

Self-images, whether negative or apparently positive, cause suffering for you and your loved ones in ways you might not have recognized until now. Luckily, it's possible to shed self-images. It's possible to become free of ego, though it's often not easy. It can be difficult to deconstruct and dissolve self-images because some of them are glued to your sense of self by the powerful adhesive of saṃskāras, unresolved past experiences that carry an emotional charge. For those particular self-images to dissolve, there needs to be healing or digestion of those unresolved past experiences. For example, if you have the self-image that no matter how hard you try, you are simply not good enough, or you're not as you should be, that self-image almost definitely was installed in childhood and there is almost definitely some childhood pain around not being loved unconditionally that needs to be digested or healed for that self-image to fall away permanently.

Thankfully, some self-images are not too strongly linked to a particular saṃskāra, in which case it is possible to look at each one and say, "That's just a thought, and I am not that thought; I'm the one who is aware that there are thoughts while already being free of them." Each self-image, seen for what it really is—a thought that has no power in and of itself—falls away or dissolves, sometimes piece by piece, sometimes all at once.

People who are engaged in activities, behaviors, and careers that align with how life naturally expresses through them find that when they shed their self-images, nothing changes much in their external lives. Everything might look pretty much the same from the outside: they don't change their job or their primary relationships, but they're experiencing it all in a whole new way. Free from the ego, they're experiencing their life as the spontaneous, ever-fresh, intrinsic joy of aliveness, expressing through the activity of the moment with no sense of obligation or burden.

By contrast, those who have created for themselves a life situation that does not reflect their real values will, upon shedding their self-images, find their life as they have known it crumbling about their ears. This transition can take a year or two. While difficult and often painful, it results in a more beneficial scenario for all concerned. You contribute to others' well-being much more effectively when you are happy, and one of the keys to happiness is shedding as much of the ego structure as you can and thereby living in a way that is a natural expression of your essence-nature.

There is Only One "Self"

I'll conclude by considering a closely related issue. These days, many people speak of "connecting to my higher self" or "receiving a download from my higher self" or similar phrases. The problem with this concept is that it reinforces the idea that your "higher self" is something distinct from you. This idea couldn't be more opposed to the teachings of Yoga or nonduality. By speaking of the putative "higher self" as something separate from you, you reinforce your identification with the constructed ego-self. This is deeply inimical and antithetical to truth-realization.

You are, and always have been, the so-called higher self. There's no magical guardian angel version of you hovering somewhere in the ether for you to receive downloads from. It's right here, right now, as you. The more you see through the falsehood of the constructed self, the more you'll be able to repose in the pure awareness-presence that you are. Reposing in your true being makes space for insights to arise from a place much deeper than your conditioned mind. Of course, such insights are then given form as words by the conditioned mind, which is why we retain a healthy skepticism as to whether they have been expressed in the most accurate way possible. When given form as words, they can only be tools, not truths. Nonetheless, they are qualitatively different from verbal formulations that are nothing but the regurgitation of conditioning. Insights that arise when we repose in pure awareness-presence have a luminous clarity that burn away the cobwebs of ordinary thought and rumination. They constitute the truth in relation to which the notion of a "download from your higher self" is a near enemy.

The key understanding here is that you don't have two selves, a higher one and a lower one. The ego, being in this view nothing but a complex mental construct, is not a self of any kind. There is only one self, and you are it. It's the awareness-presence permeating the whole of your experience right now. It's the power by which you're aware of anything at all.

CONTEMPLATIVE EXERCISE

Where Is the Self?

Get settled and take a few deep breaths. Let's do an exercise that will allow us to distinguish between self-concept and the natural "I" sense, the sense of your own being. Once you're settled, notice the thoughts you have about the self that you assume you are, the person named so-and-so. Then notice the space of awareness within which these thoughts arise. Do you notice that that space doesn't have a name, gender, or identity? That space is simple awareness-presence, always already free of conceptualization and identity. Next turn your attention to the mass of sensations you call the body. Do you notice that this mass of sensations is always already free of your thoughts about it? Do you notice that your direct experience of the body is always already free of your thoughts (and judgments) about the body? Do you notice that simple beingness suffuses the experience of bodily sensation and whatever else you're experiencing? If you have a thought about being a separate self, do you notice that beingness suffuses it in the same way it does everything else and to the same degree? Since your beingness suffuses all that you are aware of to the same degree, you're no more your thoughts about yourself than you are anything else that arises in your experience. Rest in this simple beingness. Just be the awareness-presence that you always already are.

Nonduality

THE CONCEPT OF NONDUALITY, however refined and however beautifully expressed, is always the near enemy of the nonconceptual direct experience of nonduality. Nonetheless, I'll try to explain it in a way that at least comes closer to the truth.

What is nonduality? People ask this question a lot, which is in a sense surprising because nonduality is incredibly simple. It's duality that's complicated. In fact, nonduality is precisely that which cannot be simpler. Nonduality refers to the undivided totality of immediate experience as presented in any and every moment. That is, experience without any imagined divisions whatsoever. But the fact that nonduality is extremely simple doesn't mean it's easy to explain because language is inherently dualistic. Every word has a specific meaning by negating other possible meanings.

In fact, language is a primary factor in how the mind creates the illusion of duality, especially in terms of the duality of subject versus object. There is a classic example of this in the Tantric tradition, expressed in the simple sentence "I see a pot," which implies by its grammatical structure that there are three separate things, their relation being what constitutes the sense of the sentence.

- There's a putative seer, denoted by the word *I*.
- There's a putative separate object that is seen, denoted by the word *pot*.
- There's the act of seeing that putatively links those two: "I see [a] pot."

But this is nothing more than linguistic convention. When we examine our direct experience, we don't find three things at all; we just find one thing, the conscious experience of seeing (in this case, seeing in a pot sort of way). When we examine our direct experience, we can't find a seer separate from the experience of seeing, nor can we find something seen that's separate from the experience of seeing. For most people, this becomes even more clear in the case of hearing. If you're attending to your direct experience, when you hear any given sound, like the chirp of a bird, you notice that you can't find a hearer separate from hearing, nor can you say that the sound is something separate from the hearing of it. So, in reality, there's just one thing, one consciousness event, not three things as the sentence "I hear a chirp" seems to suggest. It doesn't matter how we articulate this insight, and indeed different traditions articulate it differently since the same insight could be expressed by saying, with reference to this example, "There is only hearing" or "There is only the conscious knower, manifesting as the experience of hearing (and all other experiences)." These are both trying to point to the same nonverbal, nonconceptual insight. We don't have words designed to express the intrinsic unity of conscious experience, so there's no easy way to indicate that this epistemological triad (e.g., hearer-hearing-heard) appears as triadic solely as a function of language.

Whether you're seeing, hearing, or feeling, it's nothing but a singular consciousness event, a vibration of consciousness that you label in a particular way. Earlier I said that you can't find a hearer separate from hearing, but for some people, this point is not perfectly clear because they can imagine a separate hearer or knower. You can seemingly conjure a separate self into existence by simply imagining that an agent is needed to perform the action (as grammar seems to suggest)—that there must be a hearer to do the hearing. But when you look at your direct experience carefully, you find that this is not the case. Hearing just happens spontaneously. It's not something you do, operate, or bring about. There's no doer needed. Same for seeing, thinking, and so on. You don't do thinking. It just happens of its own accord. Thoughts arise out of nowhere, and then you take credit for them or lay claim to them, which is itself just another thought.

Without even realizing it, you constantly imagine yourself as the thinker of the thoughts. But it's just an assumption—that is to say, it's just another thought. One that is so habitual, it simply happens all the time as a matter of course, occurring at the very margins of conscious awareness, as it were. But when you look more closely, you discover that there is no thinker separate from the thoughts; there's just a space of awareness within which thoughts are arising.

Thought is a particular vibration within consciousness, just as whatever you see is nothing but light, specifically patterns of color, which are also a particular vibration within consciousness. (There's literally no such thing as color apart from your and my conscious experience of it. If you doubt me, ask any qualified neuroscientist or physicist.) If you are having a thought, just notice that the thought spontaneously arises and then at some point dissolves, giving way to another thought or silence. But there's no actual thinker of the thought in your direct experience—except in the form of yet another thought. The idea of the thinker. Same for the example of hearing—you can imagine a hearer separate from the hearing, but you don't find one in direct experience. Check it for yourself.

The Power of Belief

Some might claim to feel themselves to be the thinker of the thoughts and the experiencer of the experiences: someone to whom experience is happening. This illusion is generated by the power of belief. To take a simplistic example, if you believe that you're a terrible person, even for a moment, then you feel terrible. If you believe you're a great person, you feel great. These feelings are as ephemeral as the thoughts they are generated by, though they can be generated over and over again. In the same manner, believing yourself to be the thinker of the thoughts or the doer of the actions, generates the illusion of selfhood, the feeling of being a separate self, the insubstantiality of which is hard to notice when it's being constantly refreshed.

If you consider the matter honestly, you discover that you don't even know how to make a thought. How would you go about doing that? You don't decide what to think before you think it because if you did, you'd already be thinking it.* Be very present with direct experience, and you'll see thoughts arising of their own accord, seemingly out of nowhere. It happens as spontaneously as breathing. Like breathing, you can try to take control and direct the course of thought, but where did the impulse to do so come from? Can you claim credit for an impulse that spontaneously arises? And notice that you also can't explain why the impulse to direct the flow of thought seems compelling enough to act on sometimes and insufficiently compelling at other times. Therefore, in the phrase "You can try to take control," the word *you* is a figure of speech, an artifact of language. The impulse to take control of the course of thought arises spontaneously or not at all, and you have no say in whether it seems like an idea worth acting on or not. It just does, or it doesn't.

The illusion of a separate self, which is the agent of the actions attributed to it, has to be maintained moment to moment, and that

---

*I acquired this specific phrase from Sam Harris's discourses on the illusion of free will.

takes up a lot of energy. Most people spend a huge amount of their mental and verbal energy defending themselves, justifying themselves, and explaining themselves. When you're not busy maintaining the illusion of a separate self, you have a lot more energy at your disposal.

What are the implications of this? Well, if you explore it carefully, you find that all divisions are mind-created. They're mental constructs. Nothing in reality is divisible from anything else—"objects" constantly exchange electrons and other subatomic particles with each other, people exchange thoughts with each other, and so on, on every possible level. Information flows. There is nowhere in space-time that energy cannot transit to or from, and so reality constitutes a single indivisible whole.* Therefore, the nondual mode of perception is nothing but the whole of reality exactly as you experience it, minus your mentally imposed divisions. This sounds simple enough and it is simple, but human identity is so deeply invested in a picture of reality that depends on categorical divisions being inherently real that few people on the planet have been able to learn how to perceive in a nondual mode on demand.

The primary mental division that most of us experience is "me" versus "not me." From an early age, the persistent imagination arises that a particular bundle of phenomena is separated from everything else, that bundle of phenomena is labeled "me," and this obviously necessitates another category of "not me," which constitutes everything else—the universe, if you will. In this way you come to feel separate from the rest of reality. Some people want to know why this occurs (even though it is not necessary to answer this question to realize the truth of nonduality), and to them I would suggest an answer in the domain of evolutionary biology. It was adaptive to develop the concept and experience of a separate self, however

*The seeming exception to the rule is the collapsed stars known as black holes—but as Stephen Hawking was able to demonstrate, black holes very slowly return to the universe the energy they have swallowed, and so will eventually evaporate, after trillions of years.

illusory. We now understand that the mechanisms of biological evolution will always prioritize biological survival over and against the capacity to discern truth or reality.*

When you investigate this matter carefully, you discover that you cannot find the boundary that supposedly exists between you and everything else. As soon as you try to pin it down, it somehow slips away, even though it ordinarily seems so real. You discover that you are so inextricably embedded in your environment (physical, social, cultural, etc.) that it's most accurate to say that you are your environment in a particular configuration, just like a whirlpool is nothing but the ocean in a particular configuration. Imagined boundaries, such as that which divides you from all that is "not you," seem real because modern humans live almost entirely in a mind-world, a world constituted by imagined categories and divisions. Those categories might sometimes constitute useful tools (and other times dangerous weapons), but when you look carefully at your direct experience, prior to interpretive thought, no such categorical divisions can be found in actuality. Remove all mind-created divisions and you automatically experience wholeness. Seamless continuity of being. Oneness. And there's no separate self in it because there's no perceiver separate from perceiving.

Here I must clarify a common misunderstanding among skeptics of this view. In referring to "the nondual mode of perception," I'm not talking about a belief or the result of holding a belief. I'm not talking about the feeling that you have when you believe "We're all one" or some such thought. The stronger the belief, the stronger the corresponding feeling, but that feeling is still the product of a mental construct. Even though reality is one indivisible whole, the feeling that results from believing that proposition is something quite different from the experience of seeing it to be true independent of conceptualization.

---

*See the work of Donald Hoffman, some of which is summarized and explained in his book *The Case Against Reality.*

Mind-Created Divisions

We could put it this way: reality is whatever doesn't go away even when you stop believing in it. Therefore, the real nondual awareness or unity-consciousness is that which you experience when you stop believing in the separate self. When you can truly see, even just for a moment, all mind-created divisions as mind-created divisions, and you can see that thought has no power to create an actual division in reality, you undergo a perceptual shift so radical that words can't hope to touch it, let alone describe it.

This is why spiritual teachers like Adyashanti call awakening a "destructive process." Insight into the fundamental nature of reality can only occur through the removal of whatever obstructs that insight. It cannot be the result of acquiring new knowledge or wisdom, some missing piece of code that enables you to break through to another level of reality. That's fantasy. Nothing need be added or acquired because reality, by definition, already is what it is. The truth is always hidden in plain sight, but we fail to recognize it due to various obscuring assumptions and misunderstandings. Those are what need be dissolved and eradicated. The rest takes care of itself.

When you're experiencing in the nondual mode, it's obvious that nothing is any more "you" than anything else. The imagined difference between internal and external dissolves, and all phenomena are seen as equally internal to awareness (as indeed they are). If you have realized that awareness is what you fundamentally are (it being the only constant in the ever-changing world of experience), then it logically (and experientially) follows that all phenomena are arising within you and are you. In this mode, you don't identify with a small subset of the contents of consciousness (body and mind)—that contracted sense of identity dissolves into the totality of being, and you recognize that you are the whole of your experience. You are constituted by the totality of phenomena perceived from your vantage point, and the beingness that pervades those phenomena.

You might want to open to the possibility of seeing in this way right now. Read the next paragraph more slowly, please.

You are the totality of your experience; so, this book you're holding is no less "you" than anything else you're experiencing. The thoughts that spontaneously arise are no more "you" than the sounds that spontaneously arise in the environment. Just look at it for yourself. Isn't it the case that this physical book in your hands is just as much present within consciousness as the feeling of your body? What you call the body is a kind of sensation, and so is the feeling of the book in your hand. Sensations are vibrations within awareness. If all the sensations—body, book, chair—are equally present within awareness, how is one more "you" than another? Dissolve the imagined division within experience. Let it go. You might sense, right now, the seamless unity of being. Everything you're perceiving right now is arising within that which you are. You don't need to think about it—just notice that there's nothing separate. Everything is the substance of conscious experience. Everything is equally the substance of conscious experience.

There's nothing but phenomena arising and subsiding within the total field of awareness. You are the total field of awareness, and you are all that arises and subsides within it.

Now, one of three things just happened. If you've already seen the truth of nonduality, you effortlessly saw it again just now. It's as obvious as breathing as soon as you turn your attention to it. Or perhaps you're new to this whole nonduality thing, but just now you glimpsed, or almost glimpsed . . . something. You can't even say what, but you sensed the possibility of a whole different way of seeing and being. Or—third option—you think I'm talking nonsense, and if you just felt something strange, it was probably the result of a kind of hypnosis and nothing more. If you had the third experience, let me remind and reassure you that the nondual mode of perceiving and being doesn't require you to believe anything. It's just that the nature of language is such that anything stated in words can be interpreted as mere belief. The previous paragraphs were just a like a finger pointing to the moon; you look where the finger is pointing, and you either see the moon or you don't and that's the end of it. Later, when your vantage point has shifted again, you can look again, and perhaps you'll see it. It doesn't matter. Seeing in the nondual mode doesn't make you better or even more spiritual than anyone else, and one can be perfectly happy without it. So, in that sense, it's nothing special. For those who've experienced it, it's absolutely wondrous and nothing special at the same time. Sounds odd but it's true.

Now, some spiritual teachers who claim to be nondual teach a subtle distinction between awareness and the phenomena that arise and subside within it—or even a not-so-subtle distinction between consciousness and its contents. Making this distinction can have a heuristic value, especially in the earlier stages of the awakening process, because it helps dissolve exclusive identification with the body-mind, and that is a necessary part of the process. But ultimately, nondual awareness dissolves the distinction between consciousness and its contents that some perceive (or imagine). Then it becomes clear that all phenomena are not only vibrations within awareness but also vibrations of awareness. A sound, sensation, appearance, or feeling—it's awareness vibrating in a particular way. So, there's nothing but awareness. That's nonduality. Or rather, the nonconceptual realization of that is the real nonduality.

In conclusion, the Tantric text called Stanzas on the Recognition of the Divine says that the nondual mode of experiencing need not be interrupted by any thought or emotion. By definition, it's not incompatible with any type of experience. But when people believe otherwise, they contract out of the nondual mode as soon as a thought or emotion judged as incompatible with it arises. I would invite you to notice that when you believe a thought, you give it power and energy, you enter into its world, and you can't help but perceive things from the perspective of that thought, which is necessarily limited and often involves separation and division. And if you don't believe the thought, meaning that when you clearly see that it is just a thought and doesn't need to be believed or disbelieved, it appears as just another type of vibration within consciousness, like sensation, sound, and so on. How could any type of vibration possibly impede nondual awareness? It can't. Thoughts cannot impede or interrupt nondual awareness unless they are believed. Actively believing a thought contracts experience into the form of that thought and its associated feelings. And even then, the indivisible wholeness of being doesn't cease to be; it simply isn't visible to you from within the vantage point of the thought-world. When you believe a thought, you're entering it and seeing the world from inside it, and that's why things look different. And there's nothing inherently wrong with that, though it can cause a lot of suffering if you don't realize that that's what is happening.

If you've experienced the nondual mode of perceiving and being, you might ask, "How do I get back there?"—since most people who've experienced it regard it as a much more wonderful mode of being than the dualistic world of separation. To you I would simply say this: it will become available on demand (as it were) as soon as there nothing else you want more than truth.

Surrender

ON MANY VERSIONS OF THE SPIRITUAL PATH, we are encouraged to surrender. This is taken to mean "accept what is," and so many people interpret surrender as a kind of resignation or passivity. But in truth, resignation is the near enemy of surrender.

Etymologically, *surrender* means "to give oneself up" or "give oneself over." This is also the sense of the corresponding Sanskrit terms, *prapanna* and *ātma-nivedana,* meaning "to offer oneself to the Divine." Real surrender, I would argue, is a kind of softening and opening, a profound relaxation, because in the state of surrender, we cease all resistance to reality. We cease our argument with what is.

However, the most common misunderstanding of this is rooted in a false dualism. We imagine ourselves as something separate from the universe and thereby imagine that we are supposed to surrender or resign ourselves to this world as it is. But since we are utterly embedded in the pattern of the whole, indeed nothing but an instantiation of that very pattern, the act of surrender must include surrendering to that which life wants to do through us.

The ultimate act of surrender is one of embracing the whole of reality exactly as it is, including ourselves. But when we consider this possibility, we wrongly imagine reality as a kind of snapshot of how things are right now. Isn't this strange, considering that the most salient feature of reality is change? Embracing the whole of reality exactly as it is necessarily means embracing constant change. And the primary driver of change in our personal lives is desire.

Here we are met with a seeming paradox. How can we embrace reality as it is when we feel a natural desire to change certain things? The paradox resolves when we understand surrender as a metaprinciple. That is to say, it's perfectly possible to accept what is in this moment while simultaneously accepting our desire to change something and acting on that desire. This can be hard for the mind to understand, so I'll try to explain it a little more.

Nothing Is Wrong

In the state of surrender, we completely dissolve the belief that anything should be different from how it is. We make a sacrificial offering of this belief. We offer it up to the Divine, if you like. But this must necessarily include dissolving the belief that we shouldn't desire whatever we desire. The invitation on the spiritual path is to surrender to the whole of reality, not "surrender to all that's real except desire"! Let me offer an example of what I mean. You might feel a natural desire to fight for the rights of women in your society, help protect the environment, or raise awareness about a particular issue. Surrendering to what *is* necessarily includes honoring this activating energy we call desire. But contrary to popular belief, you don't need to believe that something is wrong to act on your desire to see a change in this world.

Surrender is an act of love, an honoring of what is. Love for what is must include your natural desire to support change (if it exists) because that desire is part of what is. Of course, most people who are activists of one sort or another are absolutely convinced that something is deeply wrong with our society, and they are engaged in a fight against the system, against the perceived wrongness. This is the salient difference I'm trying to elucidate here: someone in the state of surrender doesn't fight against anything, but they might passionately support a particular cause out of love for that aspect of reality (women, the environment, etc.). They are for something rather than against something. This is important because on the spiritual path, we come to see that hatred only begets more hatred. For example, it might seem perfectly noble and right to hate racism, but inevitably that translates to hating people who are racist, and that hatred only provokes more hatred in return, as we have seen all too well in recent years. The people who hold racist views respond to rejection and hatred by doubling down on their views. It's absolutely not the case that hating racism and loving egalitarianism are equivalent. The former adds to the total amount of hatred in our society, and the latter adds to the total amount of love.

Furthermore, the fire of hatred burns brightly but briefly in comparison to the fire of love. Love is a far more sustainable motivation than any variety of hatred. Activists for any cause who are filled with self-righteousness and anger burn out quickly, becoming cynical and embittered. But those who support a cause out of love continue to act in whatever way they can, year after year. Even if they don't see change happening in response to their actions, the love itself is nourishing. Acting on the basis of love is inherently nourishing.

Acting on the basis of love is inherently nourishing.

I understand that it might be hard to believe, but I invite you to consider the possibility that you simply don't need to believe that anything is wrong to act on your natural desire for change. Here, of course, we run into the problem of black-and-white thinking: when I refuse to assert that anything is wrong, people assume that that means I believe everything is right, that everything should be as it is, and therefore I oppose change. But this is not how it is. Embracing the whole of reality is an act of love that utterly transcends the mind-created dichotomy of right and wrong. We don't need those labels to take beneficial action.

Hatred = Resistance

Let's say you love people of all colors equally, and so you hold the value of egalitarianism. If there is an antiracism protest march in your town, you might feel moved to join it, not because you're against something but because you are for something—specifically, equal rights for all, regardless of perceived ethnicity, race, or color. While others might shout angrily, holding signs that say something like "Down with white supremacy!" you might smile happily, holding your sign that says something like "Equal rights for all!" In this scenario, you're probably smiling because it feels so nourishing to act on your natural desire.

It's impossible to be in a state of surrender and simultaneously harbor hatred in your heart because hatred is resistance to what is. But it's not impossible to be surrendered and also harbor a desire to see more equality in this world. That desire is part of what is. And since change is the most salient feature of our experience of reality, it's natural to desire change. It's also possible to love what is right now. Surrender is love for reality as it is and as it changes.

Here someone is likely to ask, "But how can I love racism?" The invitation here is to surrender to the pattern of the whole, and that can't be done in a piecemeal fashion. You're not being invited to surrender to racism, then murder, then war, etc. Our deepest heart longs to surrender to the whole of reality; it longs to fall in love with the whole pattern. In this ultimate act of love, we come to embrace our humanity in all its dimensions. With such an embrace, we see that even the worst human behavior is rooted in fundamental motives that are understandable and even honorable. For example, people naturally want to protect their family, and by extension, they naturally want to protect what they see as their tribe. If they believe, however falsely, that their tribe is in danger, then that belief might lead to extreme actions at the expense of those perceived as other (e.g., Nazis in the 1940s, Hutu people in Rwanda in the 1990s, or white supremacists in the United States today). This is love appearing in the form of hatred due to false beliefs. War is simply an extreme example of the same phenomenon. Putin invaded Ukraine out of a twisted version of love for Russian people and Russian heritage—a love that is severely distorted by false beliefs. (Here I'm oversimplifying of course; I don't mean to imply that love for his own megalomaniacal ego was not also a factor.) These comments are not intended to justify the actions in question. Rather, I seek to show that those who you find it easy to hate and condemn are acting because of the same fundamental motivations that motivate your own actions. When you see that this is true, you can only hate the other if you hate yourself.

Here I don't mean to suggest that the state of surrender is one in which we are happy about all that is. In fact, in the surrendered state, it's natural to grieve human suffering. It's just that we no longer see suffering as something wrong, something that shouldn't be. The perception of wrongness is not possible in the surrendered state, but plenty of things are worthy of grief. Grief is a natural part of what is.

The state of surrender to reality is a state of clear seeing, in which we see that thoughts are just thoughts. The thought that something shouldn't be how it *is* is meaningless because what is already is, and the thought that something should be different is merely a justification for an already-existent desire for change, which in fact needs no justification.

You might notice that I used the phrase "natural desire." Does this imply that there are unnatural desires? Not exactly. That phrase serves to distinguish those desires that arise innately, as opposed to desires that arise based on a thought. If you believe that your success is contingent on someone else's failure, you might want to sabotage that person—but this is not a natural desire. If the belief ceases, the desire evaporates. By contrast, our desires for human connection, belonging, security, and so on are not dependent on a belief.

Having said all this, I must also acknowledge that however well I explain the principle of surrender and its ramifications, it will always be possible to misinterpret this teaching in potential harmful ways. This is so because, fundamentally, embracing the whole of reality is a nonrational act that cannot be explained in conceptual terms. It's the deepest longing of the spiritual heart, and once it occurs, everything makes perfect sense in a crystal clear, nonconceptual way that is always impossible to communicate perfectly to one for whom it has not yet occurred.

Radical Self-Acceptance

Let us turn now to the more personal aspect of the teaching on surrender. This embrace of the whole of reality as it is and as it changes necessarily includes radical self-acceptance, as already hinted at above. Radical self-acceptance is (in part) founded on the clear insight that you are a child of the universe, and the universe couldn't have gotten it wrong. There is nothing wrong with you, and there never was. And if you have a natural desire to change some aspect of your behavior, that's not wrong, either. If the desire is based on love, rather than self-hatred, it cannot fail to come to fruition. With radical self-acceptance, which is an aspect of surrender to reality as it is, we love ourselves as we are and as we change. This is something much deeper than self-approval. There are aspects of you that don't necessarily merit approval, but the whole of what you are merits unconditional love, which thankfully transcends the mind-created dichotomy of approval versus disapproval. Your worth and value is proven by your very existence, and it needs no other proof. Your contribution to the universe lies in simply being yourself. Every human life is a thread in the pattern, and every thread is required to make the pattern.

How did you ever get the idea that something is wrong with you as you are? Every sense of your own inadequacy or wrongness is nothing but internalized cultural programming. People judged your behavior from the time you could understand language in accordance with their culturally conditioned normative views, and that is what generated your baseless self-hatred and self-criticism.

Radical self-acceptance is not the cumulative result of accepting one part of yourself after another in a piecemeal fashion. It happens all at once, when you see that thoughts aren't the sorts of things that can be true and the perception of wrongness in yourself is nothing but a thought.

Radical self-acceptance does not prevent us from receiving others' feedback. Quite the contrary. Egoic self-approval is what inhibits our receptivity to feedback. When we accept ourselves exactly as we are (and as we change), we can hear others' feedback without becoming defensive. We are curious about the unintended impact of our actions because we're open to growth and new understanding, that being a natural part of our humanity. You never need to believe anything is wrong with you to be open to the possibility of change. Change is natural and inevitable, so it doesn't require such a belief as its basis. When others are hurt by your words or actions, it's not bad or wrong; it's an opportunity to learn about how things land for them and about the possible consequences of your words and actions. When misunderstandings and unintended consequences and pain are all a natural part of being human, why would we make any of them wrong? Some of them are worthy of grieving, surely, but that's doesn't make them wrong. That doesn't mean they shouldn't have happened. Haven't you noticed that humans don't usually learn or grow without the prompting of pain? Could it be that there's no mistake in all this?

Some people imagine that a state of radical surrender to reality would mean never asking others to change their behavior in any way. But if the urge to invite someone to make a change naturally bubbles up in you, being surrendered to reality means there's nothing to inhibit you in articulating that invitation. As soon as it's given, you're ready to surrender to whatever happens next. Of course, this only works if the invitation is not based on a judgmental thought that the other person should be different from how they are—in this paradigm, the invitation is based on the desire to give the other person the opportunity to contribute to your well-being. For example, you might say, "Hey, when you talk really fast, I tend to get a little anxious. Would it be possible for you to slow down a bit? It would help me be more relaxed, if so." And in the paradigm of surrender to reality, you're willing to hear a no to your request. Having heard a no, you might choose to spend less time with that person if that's what feels right for you—all while being free of the belief that they should be different from how they are. Such freedom is a truly wondrous thing.

Surrender, then, is nothing but the radical act of embracing reality as it is (and as it changes): softening and giving up our argument with what is. Seeing that nothing is wrong with how things are ("wrong" being a culturally contingent mental construct) while not negating our desires to make changes, either. Surrender is embracing the whole of reality, without exception. When we see surrender as problematic, it's because we're leaving something out of our embrace of the whole. For example, when someone's behavior makes you want to say, "Hey, that's not okay!" you can say it, even while knowing that at the deepest level, everything's always okay. There's not a hair out of place anywhere in the universe. There couldn't be. And if your rational mind can't accept that statement, I invite you to notice that essence-nature, your innate beingness, already perfectly accepts your mind's nonacceptance. In this teaching, we're not trying to force the mind to surrender to reality. That would be both futile and paradoxical. We're seeking instead to access that deepest level of our being, on which embracing the whole of reality as it is (and as it changes) is the most natural thing of all.

There's one more element of this that we need to acknowledge here: the fact that what we can accurately know about reality is infinitesimal compared to all that we don't know or aren't sure of. So, when we surrender to reality, we are necessarily surrendering to the great unknowing, as I like to call it. Though it's possible to directly sense the elegance, symmetry, and balanced harmony of the pattern as a whole, we cannot know all the details, the vast majority of the threads of that pattern. It is the mind that parses details, and our tiny minds are dwarfed and humbled by the immensity of detail in this observable universe. When that truth is seen, the great unknowing is sensed, and that sensing can be frightening or overwhelming. For example, you absolutely don't know what's going to happen in your own life one year from now, let alone further down the road. You might know that A and B are more likely than X and Y, and on that basis, you might project a comfortable picture of the future so you can feel more secure, in which case you might be blindsided by reality. Just as life is not your story about it, the future is not your projected image of it. Literally anything could happen. To be in true surrender to reality, we must become at ease with the great unknowing. This takes time. It can't be rushed, but it helps to acknowledge to ourselves every day that almost everything is unknown: when loved ones will die, which plans will work and which will go south for unforeseen reasons, when breakthroughs will happen, when governments will crumble, and so on. When we arrive at acceptance of this unknowing, when we're finally content to dwell in don't-know mind, it's a profound relief. We have finally arrived at true surrender, the state of not resisting any aspect of reality, and in that state, we can fully

To be in true surrender to reality, we must become at ease with the great unknowing.

appreciate the incredible beauty of life, with all its joy, banality, and tragedy. We see life like an exquisitely beautiful painting: the light and shadow are equally part of its beauty.

CONTEMPLATIVE EXERCISE

Melting Resistance into Openness

—

Though you can't ever make yourself surrender, you can practice melting resistance into openness. Please sit comfortably and take a few deep breaths. Once you're settled, notice what aspect of your experience you're resisting today, whether that resistance is subtle or obvious. Surround your resistance with gentle openness. Let it be as it is. Surround it with love, if you can. Then, little by little, let the knot of resistance unravel. Let it soften. Let it melt. Tears, a deep breath, or a sigh may come. As the body opens and relaxes, simply become the openness. Breathe as pure openness. Let whatever wants to move through you move through. Just continue to be the openness through which the energy moves. There's nothing to grab on to, and nothing to resist. Openness does neither. You already are that openness. In this state, perhaps you can see the beauty of what is, feel grateful for what is, or laugh at yourself. Or all of these. Then rest as pure, quiet openness. Let it be a blessing.

ACKNOWLEDGMENTS

The germ of the idea for this book came many years ago from Jody Greene, Professor of Literature, Feminist Studies, and the History of Consciousness at UC Santa Cruz. Their wisdom and compassion nurtured my earliest stirrings of real insight on the spiritual path. The topic of near enemies of the truth as reimagined in this book was fleshed out in many conversations with the members of my wonderful community to whom I owe the deepest debt of gratitude for their love, insight, and endless support. (You can join us, if you like, at learn.tantrailluminated.org.) That community includes my partner Skye, who has been the biggest support of all during the period of writing this book. And of course, I would have nothing of value to offer those on the spiritual path were it not for my beloved teachers, who gave me everything, and without whom I would not be alive today.

INDEX

A

B

C

D

E

F

G

H

I

J

K

O

P

Q

R

S

T

ABOUT THE AUTHOR

Christopher D. Wallis, PhD, also known as Hareesh, is a Sanskritist and scholar-practitioner of Classical Tantra with thirty years of experience. He was initiated by a traditional Indian guru at the age of sixteen, and received education at yoga ashrams, both in India and the West.

Hareesh is the founder of tantrailluminated.org, an online learning portal where he teaches classical Tantric philosophy and Tantric practices, meditation, and Sanskrit to an engaged community of practitioners. He also offers in-person workshops, retreats, and classes in Portugal and around the world.

Hareesh is the author of *Tantra Illuminated: The Philosophy, History, and Practice of a Timeless Tradition* and *The Recognition Sutras: Illuminating a 1,000-Year-Old Spiritual Masterpiece.* He holds a BA in Religion and Classics from the University of Rochester, an MA in South Asian Studies from UC Berkeley, an MPhil in Classical Indian Religions from Oxford, and a PhD in Sanskrit from UC Berkeley. He lives with his partner in Figueiró dos Vinhos, in Central Portugal, and Boulder, Colorado.

Hareesh.org
Tantrailluminated.org